NOT QUITE ITHAKA

Encounters on the Way

Other Publications by Keith Harrison

Collections of Poetry
Points in a Journey
Songs from the Drifting House
The Basho Poems
The Complete Basho Poems
A Burning of Applewood (Selected Poems)
Changes (New & Collected Poems 1962–2002)

Translations
Catullus: At the Wedding of Peleus and Thetis (with Linda Clader)
Sir Gawain and the Green Knight

Radio Play
The Water Man

Theatre
The Papers of Lady Ann Vaughn

Text
How to Stop Your Papers from Killing You (and Me)

CD
When We Come Home: Poems and Songs

Forthcoming
My Father's Apples: *New Poems & Late Pickings*
Once Upon a River: Essays on Liberal Learning
Rhythm and Desire: Essays on the Art of Poetry
The Papers of Lady Ann Vaughn (play text)
Time of the Goat (novel)

KEITH HARRISON

NOT QUITE ITHAKA

Encounters on the Way

A Memoir

BLACK
WILLOW
PRESS

NORTHFIELD, MINNESOTA
CANBERRA, AUSTRALIA

Except for short excerpts in articles and reviews, permission to re-print any material must be obtained by writing to the author at Black Willow Press.

ISBN 978-0-939394-21-0

Second Revised Printing

Cover photo by Jillian Foehn
Book design by Mark F. Heiman

Editorial note: The author's British-style punctuation and spellings have been intentionally retained rather than Americanised.

ACKNOWLEDGEMENTS

It's been very helpful to test a number of these pieces in various places. The audience at Manning Clark House and its then director, Kerrie Nelson, gave me valuable encouragement as did those who attended a reading at *The Inner Artist*, Woodend, kindly arranged by Shane Bartley. At Christmas, 2020, in the Victorian Alps thirteen members of the Gibson family were very generous and helpful in their comments, as have been friends and family in Minnesota and a number of colleagues at Carleton College. Many have pushed me hard to finish the project, and their promptings have been very helpful, especially at times when my attention was hijacked by a host of other demands. My warm thanks to everyone involved.

Thanks also to my niece Jillian Foehn for the photograph in the cover design and to Rachel Alexandra for the portrait on the back cover. The electronic wizardry and editing skills of Mark Heiman have once again saved the day. He has guided both me and the text through complex problems that I'd thought insoluble. He deserves, and has, my warmest thanks.

Various well-loved friends and relations who have been a significant part of my days, to my disappointment, did not find their way into these pages. Whatever peculiar rhythm this work possesses, their stories belong in another place and will, with luck, appear when the time is ripe.

Black Willow Press, Mark Heiman and the author gratefully acknowledge the support, and the financial assistance of Dean Beverley Nagel and the Trustees of Carleton College in connection with the publication of this book.

I have been so firmly and affectionately encouraged by Jenny Gibson to complete this project that, without her insistence and her many editorial suggestions, it may not have appeared. My gratitude for her support, is something for which it is difficult to find adequate expression.

Hackberry Hollow, Northfield, Minnesota
& Ainslie, ACT, Australia, 1991–2022

…Then, when you're old, your heart and mind
brimming with all you've encountered on the way,
not expecting Ithaka to offer more,
drop anchor at the island…

from *Ithaka*, by C. P. Cavafy

[The painter] Bryullov one day corrected a pupil's study. The pupil, having glanced at the altered drawing, exclaimed: 'Why, you only touched it a tiny bit, but it is quite another thing.' Bryullov replied: 'Art begins where the tiny bit begins.'

from the notebooks of Leo Tolstoy, 1870

for Jenny and Katrina

and in memory of
Inger Christina Götesdotter Harrison, 1939–2019
and Anna Rebecca Harrison, 1969–2021

in your honour
I too will something make and joy in the making

FOREWORD

Perhaps one way of looking at this collection of sketches and vignettes is to think of them as a gathering of paintings in an exhibition by the same artist. Though they're sometimes connected, that connection is not a linear one and the pieces don't form a continuous story, as in some autobiographies. Another way might be to think of them as a kind of musical experiment in different modes of prose. To alter my metaphor once again: I think I must have carried with me, subconsciously as I wrote, the notion of 'spots of time' that Wordsworth used in his long autobiographical poem, *The Prelude*.

Our strongest memories recur to us as flashes, vivid and unannounced. I have therefore cast this book in the present continuous tense. To emphasize the idea of continuity in our *acts* of remembering, as distinct from the *facts* of our experience, I've also excised the original one-word 'chapter' titles I used in the early drafts. In those drafts I set down my recollections in the order in which they occurred, and paid little attention to chronology. Later, I sensed that such an arrangement could lead to what Yvor Winters called 'the fallacy of imitative form' and cause unnecessary confusion. So now there's a loose chronology, beginning with the first things I can remember and ending in the ongoing pandemic, though that chronology is, again, not a strict one. Nor have I made any attempt at being comprehensive because I don't really know what a comprehensive account of one's life might be. The 'subject' and, so to speak, the 'object', keep changing, and there's no end to those changes until we are no longer here.

CONTENTS

ILLUSTRATIONS

1
Brothers in War

THE SILENCE INSIDE THE LIGHT that floods through the white curtains is all around us while I stand beside my mother's chair which was rocking and isn't rocking now and in her lap she has what she calls her knitting though she's not knitting now because her hands are still. There's no one else in the house and we're alone in the light. Perhaps the light and the silence are going to tell us why we're here. I can't, so I stand beside her while we listen to each other's breathing and wait for the silence to say something.

MR. CLUTTERBUCK HAS A BIG NOSE and when he picks me up it spikes me in the neck and he says 'tick-tock' and he laughs so much it hurts my ears. Then Mrs. Clutterbuck puts her arms around me and she says 'tick-tock' and my mother comes into the room and they're all laughing so much they can't speak and Bosun, the brown dog, barks and bangs his tail against their legs.

'I CAN COUNT TO TEN', says David, who is my brother.
'And I can count to nine', I say.
'Well do it', Dad says. 'You start, David'.

David rattles the numbers off straight to up to ten, and glares at me and I race up to nine and stop and they all laugh at me, and shout TEN, and I shout TEN back at them.

Then my father looks at David and asks him, 'All right, what's 8 plus 8?'

My brother looks down into his bowl of corn-flakes and doesn't answer and I shout 'SIXTEEN', and this time they don't laugh but try to pretend it didn't happen.

I go to the bathroom and I say to myself *That was a guess because I don't really know that 8 and 8 make sixteen, but I got it right.*

It seems to me a good idea to keep that secret, and I do.

SOMETIMES THEY CALL MR. CLUTTERBUCK *Wolf*, sometimes *Wolfie*. He points his nose round the door and into the room, and then follows it in. The nose stays out in front of him everywhere he goes, and it swivels about as if he's looking for it. When he finds it he pokes it into the back of my neck, and says 'So, what does Tick-tock say?' And I say 'tick-tock' and they laugh again and again. My mother makes tea and we all have Anzac biscuits but I only have a little bit which my mother breaks off for me. Wolfie and Mrs. Clutterbuck live next door but they're always here wanting to bounce me around on their knees. I don't understand Mrs. Clutterbuck whose big teeth shine, and I don't understand Wolfie whose long nose drips unless he grabs it with his handkerchief, and holds it hard while he loudly snorts the drips away. It sounds like a huge truck roaring along the road.

David and Keith harrison, 1934

IT SHINES LIKE AN EGG-TOMATO and every time I pass it I want to pluck if off and bite it hard. One day she sees me standing there, staring. 'Son, that thing's called a chili and it's terribly, terribly hot. It's nothing like a tomato, son. Don't touch it.' My mother might know everything but my mother isn't me and one day on my way to the outdoor dunny I grab it and bite it hard. It's as if someone's shoved a burning stick down my throat and I hurl the chili down in the dirt and run inside screaming. There's no one around and I keep screaming. My mother comes out of a dark room in the back of the house: *'I told you, never, never, never…'*

Then she takes me to the sink and pours some water and makes me sluice it into my mouth but the flames in my throat get even hotter and I'm still screaming until she pours me cold milk in a glass and forces me to swallow and now I feel a bit better and the fire in my mouth begins to seep away, but it's very slow.

THIS MORNING I FOUND a way to trick him. The idea is to head for the gate and just as he's about to catch me from behind I'll grab the top bar and swing it shut very fast so that he'll crash into it. *That will stop him,* I say to myself, *that will really stop him.* But I have to work on it. I know I can run faster than he does so I have to pretend he's catching me, and then do it. That afternoon, after school, when no one's watching, I practise. I sprint around the garden slowing down a bit as I get to the gate. I leave the gate a little open and, as I go through, quickly pull it shut with my left hand. *It will work, I know it will.* Next day, I pick a fight, or he does—it's all the same—and he chases me out of the house and into the garden. We race around the path and through the gate three times and I let him almost catch me, then as we go through the gate for the fourth time and I feel him come really close, I do it. I slam the gate shut and his whole body bangs against it hard. I hear him grunt and cry out and I keep running. He's still sitting there, holding his chest when I come back a few minutes later and run straight past him into the kitchen.

ALISON IS MY COUSIN and because she's a girl she's more beautiful than I will ever be. I want to wear her shoes and can't, I want to talk like her because she says her words in a special way and her words are very clear. She has large white teeth and they're beautiful too, and her yellow dress swirls around her legs and I look down and see my own dirty shoes and I want to throw them away and that night as I lie rolling about in the heat trying to sleep I tell myself that when I wake up my body will be smooth and the bulge down there where I do my pissing will be gone and I will be exactly the same as my cousin Alison, who has nothing down there and then I find myself awake and the bulge hasn't gone and I have to go on just the way I am.

I want to get next to my brother.
 Garn, get back, I'm first.
I want to get next to my brother.
 Garn! I tighten my fist

and smack the face. My brother
 says 'That's Ronnie Salt, and
what did you hit him for?'
 There's warm blood on my hand.

WHEN HE SQUATS ON ME and tries to squeeze the breath out of my chest I have an even better trick and he always forgets: I shoot my legs up his back over his shoulders and hook my heels on his chin. Then I straighten my legs so quickly that I ram the back of his head down on the floor. He should know better. He's tried it several times and I always do it. I'm never sure if he's trying to kill me before I can kill him. If he isn't trying to kill me I shouldn't bang his head on the floor so hard, but I'm not sure about that. I'm not sure at all.

FOR SOME REASON I'M IN A TRENCH they're digging for a sewer-pipe and the clay's sticking to my sand-shoes. Uncle Alf, who can't stop playing practical jokes on us, comes out of the house and stands on the edge of the trench. He reaches in his pocket and pulls out a small black box with hinges, hands it to me and says:

'Happy Six, son!' Then he turns back toward the house.

I open the box and find a brand new mouth-organ. I put it to my lips and blow and find to my delight that I can play it immediately, and soon I'm sending *Men of Harlech* and *Yankee Doodle* into the tall country air. There's no one listening and that's just what I want. Later on I'm given a larger instrument with a key on the end that makes all kinds of new sounds but right now this plain Höhner is just fine.

After a while Uncle Alf re-appears.
— Good on you, son. I knew you could make it work.

He borrows it from me, wipes it and begins to play music with very fast runs.

I tell him I heard Larry Adler playing some of those on the radio, and say, 'Jeez, I wish I could play like that.'
— That's where I got them. From Larry Adler.
— But how did you learn to do it?
— Dunno. Like you did just now, I suppose. You just play.

HELENE IS OUR SISTER and she's got a needle in her heel. Yesterday the Japanese bombed Darwin and Helene has a needle. In the dark afternoon a wind rode up the Hawkesbury Valley and ripped the roof from a house a mile away and dropped it on our road and Helene has a needle deep in her heel because she trod on it hard and it hit the bone and broke off and she's only three and David and I are crying because they've taken her away. When the wind pulled the roof high in the air over our house and let it go it was like something dropping through deep water. It spun in the white-blue air above the paddock, then seemed to hang there a long while. Then it crashed onto the road.

All day wind thrashes itself in the tree by the tennis-court, then the rains come, and Helene's still in hospital when the lights come on and we look out at the black pools that hold the streetlights waiting for any sign of an ambulance that will bring her home. Helene is our sister and she's only three and the needle's still in her heel and it's broken off and she's not coming home tonight.

The author's mother, Jess Harrison, ca. 1960

RIGHT NOW ALL WE KNOW is that the air is pale blue and already half on fire and the grass in the paddock is dead brown. In the bathroom the floor-tiles are deliciously cold under our feet, so cold that last night I crept from my bed in the first light, twisted about on a hot blanket, and finally slept there.

After breakfast Mother will take us to the river again and we'll sit in the water all day while Dad fights fires near a place called Penrith where I've never been. He'll come back covered in ash, as he did yesterday, his eyes blinking white, a stranger with singed hair, a silent man, crumpled with fatigue.

The author's father, harvey harrison, ca. 1960

A day of cloud and the grey Hawkesbury
winding under the bridge, and four
kids waist-deep in the slow water
squinting in the noon's glare.

Laughing, he grabs my legs, and I
strike out, and move away. He's followed,
watching; trips me again, and we wrestle
fiercely, flop about, and break — to brood

apart. But when he charges and
dumps me, I swallow mud
and a white madness flares — and I
clutch him, pressing his head

down on the sand in the thrashed water.
He can't wriggle when I squat
over his chest, and his eyes roll,
wide with fear and hate

as I force him down. And I will
kill you, brother — but for this man with hard
hands wrenching me off, yelling,
Want to drown him, you young bastard?

A day of cloud and the grey Hawkesbury
winding under the bridge, and four
kids waist-deep in the slow water
squinting in the noon's glare.

'CLINKER-BUILT, MARCONI RIG', DAVID TELLS ME, showing off, but today we're not sailing, we're rowing. Three oars to starboard, two to port. A solid boat weighing over a ton. We pull her out to the starting buoy in the Lane Cove River, Charlie Lithgow at the helm, making us keep strict time. If you catch a crab or don't get the stroke right Charlie gives you hell.

The harbour water's choppy and we have to guess the wave-heights, or grab empty air. Arms and backs on fire we row the measured mile in good time. 'Do that on Saturday, and you'll win', Charlie says.

We haul the boat up on the slips and go inside and dress in our bell-bottoms, tunics and navy hats. We're only cadets but big enough to be mistaken for regular Navy so that the cox of the liberty-boat at Circular Quay doesn't question us when we ask him to take us to the *Indomitable*, a huge British aircraft carrier at anchor off Garden Island. They even pipe us onto the quarter-deck, where we salute the officers in their white uniforms and gold braid.

We climb the gangway to the flight-deck, which suddenly drops, and we go down and down into the hangars—it seems like ten floors. Here, below the water-line we meet the sailors in their smelly quarters. Their voices are rough, with accents we've heard on the radio—West Country, Scots, Cockney. We're in time for lunch which, today, is a huge tray of plum-duff.

There are no plates. The men simply surround the tray and plunge spoons into it. They have to dodge each other among the hammocks that hang between the bulk-heads. It smells as if everyone here's been farting for days and there's no ventilation. The scene's repulsive as they drip saliva and mucous into the mess of stewed plums and pastry that they call their lunch. David and I watch, fascinated, feeling sick.

Later we go to the quartermaster's store and buy cigarettes — *Capetown to Cairo, Senior Service, Wild Woodbine* — sixpence
a pack, one and three-pence for fifty. We stuff them in our hats
and the calves of our long socks, into the deep pockets of our
jerkins. On the way to Wynyard underground David tells me I
should give three packets to Dad, and I get angry. 'I gave him
three last week, and you only gave him two.' He turns away as
the train screams into the station and runs along the platform,
three or four carriages away from mine. 'You stink', he yells as
he jumps on board, and I'm glad to be alone. *He's a mean bastard*,
I say to myself, and the train jumps forward, as if to punctuate
what I'm thinking.

At Homebush the train waits for a minute, then five, then ten.
Police on the platform, a hubbub of low voices, torches flashing.
I sit for a while, then feel my stomach tensing. Something has
happened to my brother. I jump off the train, which shows no
sign of moving and see him, whey-faced, in the light from the
waiting-room. He grabs my arm. 'Jesus, son, there's something
awful along there', he says.

— What?
— You don't want to see it.
— Why not?
— It'll make you sick.

I ignore him and hurry along the platform where a crowd of
people and a few policemen are peering through a carriage window. At first, in the dim light, I don't notice anything, then I see
a man propped up, rather stiffly, in the corner near the window.
He's wearing a cheap grey pin-stripe suit, but the odd thing
about him is that above his collar there's only a short piece of
bone poking up, and no head. As my eyes become adjusted and
I look around I see what my brother means. The mess on the
walls and floor looks like someone went mad with a paint-brush

and there's thick red paint with bits of yellow and bone-shluck on the walls and floor, and all over the seat. I begin to gag. My brother pulls me away. We're still simmering from our quarrel but it all drops away now, and I can feel him there in the dark beside me, trying to be kind to his kid brother.

— Mum'll be furious, he says. We're over an hour late.

The death-train pulls out and in half an hour another one comes to take us home. We tell Mother and Dad the story, highly edited, eat in silence and go to bed in our garage sleep-out.

For a horrible moment, waiting alone in that motionless train, when I heard all the movement on the platform, I thought I'd lost my brother and almost shat my pants. Now I can hear him breathing regularly as he falls into his sleep, and though I don't say anything, I'm grateful for the regularity of that sound.

2
Music, Words and Grandpa

Christopher John harrison. ca. 1946

Lillian Caroline harrison. ca. 1946

—WHAT'S THAT YOU'RE READING, son? Asks my cousin John.

— *Biggles,* I say. *Biggles in Africa.*

— Well, that's okay, but it's kid's stuff and you want to get beyond that now.

— What do you suggest I read instead?

— There are plenty of good books. The real fun's finding them for yourself. Ayway, I brought something special for you to hear today.

He takes a record from its sleeve and puts it on the gramophone. I've never heard anything like it. It's fresh and intensely alive.

— What's that? I ask.

— It's called *Eine Kleine Nachtmusik,* and it's by Mozart. I'll bring some more music next week.

All that day I can't get the sounds and rhythms out of my head. No one composed this music. It just seemed to happen.

DAD'S AT WORK. We're in the kitchen and mother says: 'This is difficult for you boys, and it's difficult for all of us, but now the war's over we have… we have to go to Melbourne. Your Dad has a new job in the Air Force base down there.'

I can tell she's been crying.

'Helene and I'll stay here for a few days to clean things up and pack and you'll both go ahead of us on the train with Dad. I'll join you in a few days when Dad finds a house.'

All the way to Melbourne Dad says almost nothing. We know he's worried but he doesn't share any of his concerns with us. We stay one night in a hotel and then he tells us he's found a house: 'One of the few left in Melbourne', he says. 'We're really lucky.'

When we get inside the house he still says nothing but later tells us we mustn't open the door to anyone until he gets back in the evening. 'It's important that you stay inside. There's food in the kitchen and you've got plenty of books.'

Next day when he leaves for work he doesn't explain why we have to stay inside.

In a few days Mother and Helene arrive from Sydney and we settle in. My brother and I have new bunk-beds and we can't get used to them. We feel each others' movements all the time and we can't sleep.

This is nothing like the big farm-house we had in Windsor or the garage sleep-out in Concord West. This is Melbourne where it seems the houses and the rooms are small.

I DON'T EVEN KNOW WHAT 'homo' means. To me, he's simply a fat man with a gold tooth and an ability to draw music out of us, an ability which has everyone wondering, including himself. Today it's a chorus from Haydn's *Creation* and this is my first day in this class and this school which is very different from the one in Sydney.

After the Haydn, which the boys sing confidently in several parts, we have time to hear some pieces from our classmates. One gives us a jazzy rag on the harmonica, another an Irish fiddle-tune. Then the fat teacher with one gold tooth turns to the curly-headed kid beside him:

— Well, Geoffrey, your turn now. What do you have for us?
— It's a piece called *Czardas* I've been working on for a week.

He snugs the flute-tubes together, blows down them to warm the metal and produces a sound like a wuffling whistle. No one laughs. We're all genuinely interested.

Later on I learn that good musicians consider *Czardas* a pretty ordinary piece but right now I'm completely held by the sound that seems to come not *from* Geoffrey, but *through* him. He's 14 but he plays with the skill of someone much older. He plays as if this is the only way a sensible person would spend his time. What else is there but this running language, this quick bird-flight of silvery notes, leaping about the room? And while he plays his face is intent and I notice the vein on his forehead swelling into a knotty blue rope, but there's no sense of effort in his playing.

The flute-sound takes away all the noise we usually live in, and here I am in this new school, back in the strange city where I was born 14 years ago, back from the north where we went so Dad could play his part in the war, and I'm listening to a flute. I'm also learning a queer game called Aussie Rules and when I kick the ball all my class-mates laugh because I can't do it prop-erly and my kick turns into what they call a 'toer'.

The war's over. For a few seconds in this square room with its rows of desks I have a feeling of being at home.

The boys in the class really like Geoffrey D'Ombrain. He's the genuine thing and we elect him class leader. Today he plays *Czardas* for anyone who wishes to listen and Mr. Collie, with his gold tooth and little paunch, smiles a little wistfully and says 'That was a week well spent, Geoffrey — don't you think, boys?' We all clap. There's no faking. 'Good on you, Dommie!', then we file out the door, to Geography and Woodwork, to jostling and yelling and football, to the hot scrum of our un-musical lives.

ONE THING'S CERTAIN: if you run as fast as you can and hit the middle of the board you'll go up, and up and you'll leap a long way. I can see them standing down there beside the pit waiting for me. This is our final jump and there are three of us competing. I have some friends down there and some enemies too who'd like to see me break my head. I lace my spikes tighter and stretch a bit, then put my right foot on the mark I made earlier in the dust when the yard was empty, and then I swing into it and sprint toward the pit faster than I've ever done and this time I hit the board dead centre. Buildings at the edge of the field fall away then jump up suddenly and I'm rolling in the pit and someone has a tape and Mr. Stevens with his shirt undone and fat belly leans over and measures and calls out '18 foot six and a quarter. I think that's a new record!' I can feel the silence of the boys around the pit. It's a silence I don't know how to read.

No one in the street. All I have to do is buy a packet of cereal, a pint of milk and some tomatoes. Sunday morning. The lawn-mowers are still sleeping, and their owners on the verandah are hiding behind their Sunday papers. They occasionally peer out, take their tea-cups in their fingers, then retreat again behind their paper screens.

Gold light slants through the gaps in the paper-barks and pepperinas and across the tiles of houses as I walk up Short Street, round the corner into Elwyn. As I pass No. 7, a house I don't know, I pause. It seems as if a whole orchestra is pouring its sound through the front door and out into the tall, blue air. Without even thinking about it, I sit down on the fence and give my whole attention to the sound. Now it's streaming straight through me: strong, woody cellos and the basses booming like surf in a cave. I think I've heard this somewhere before but it's also totally new to me. A resonance of horns as if from the height of a castle wall. It is all very joyful and it awakens a strange emotion in me. I can't even think of walking away from it to fetch the groceries. For ten minutes I'm lost in the music and I know as I listen that, from now on, I will never be quite the same.

When it's over, I get up quickly from the fence and run to the shop, and back home. Mother says 'That took a long while, son', but I don't answer. What can I say? I don't want to explain: *I heard something which seems to have changed everything*, and be told, once again 'You're a rum fellow, son. I don't know what we can do about you.'

I don't want anything to be done about me. What I want is to know who wrote that music and where I can get it. It seems a totally sensible thing to want. I ask my cousin, John, who's visiting from Sydney and who knows about these things. I hum the main theme. 'Beethoven' he says. 'No. 6, the Pastoral. That movement's sometimes called *Peasants' Merrymaking*. I think it's the Third.'

I go to a city store and with my saved pocket money buy the four heavy acetate records. Klemperer, the Berlin Philharmonic. All the names have a curious glow in my mind. I also buy the pocket score and can hardly wait for the tram to get me home so I can plunge into this new world.

I play the music over and over, following the score. It all seems a kind of magic. How can one person hold all that in his mind? Yet the music's totally human. It's not cold or distant. Later, I buy the Beethoven 3rd and 4th piano concertos: Gieseking and Kempf, and also the scores; and Mozart's Haffner Symphony. I learn book-binding and, with great respect, make homes, with red and black spines, for my records. Dad listens to my music too. They soon become his music, and I say nothing about my discovery because I want him to believe it's his.

In our house a new rule comes into being. When this kind of music's playing we're encouraged not to talk because our talk is mostly noise. Music is for being still, and listening, and when you chatter while it's playing you sound like a fool.

SAL'S HAIR SMELLS OF FLOWERS and when I walk her home after choir-practice I want to get closer so I can smell it better. She thinks that's okay and we lean together against the paling fence with a big bush between ourselves and the kitchen window so her mother can't see us while we're kissing, which we do again and again. We know her mother's anxious but the kissing seems to take our worries away so we stay there a long time. After a while Sal pushes me away, lightly and firmly.

— What are you doing for the holidays?

I don't want to talk yet but I say 'I don't know. I'd like to go to the beach or something.'

I try to pull her toward me again but she locks her arms and holds me away.

— I've got an idea.
— What?
— Well, my uncle lives in Woodend and Mum and I were going to visit him but Mum's a bit sick and she can't go. You could go instead. He's looking for someone to help him on the farm. I think we can arrange it.

That night she calls her uncle Norm and aunt Phyll in Woodend near Hanging Rock, and next Saturday I'm going there to spend a week on their farm.

THE REASON FOR THE KIND of football they play here is to fly, if only for a second, to fly as high as you can and pluck the ball out of the air. It's really the only thing worth playing for. The rest is all fumbles and grunts and banging into bodies and some of the bodies smell. The only reason you don't reach the sun as you fly is because you have a body and it's heavy so you have to imagine yourself without it and you can do it for about a second and, when you do, you take off and when you grab the ball, even if you stumble as you hit the ground you've brought back something valuable, so you kick it on to someone else.

'BLOODY SQUAWKER!' NORM SAYS, and disconnects the clip from the battery-radio which he's brought to life specially for me. With that, the Melbourne Symphony Orchestra and Elizabeth Schwarzkopf, not to say the whole history of classical music, are banished into oblivion.

Norm's the only man I've seen who can sit at table in a blue work-singlet and look graceful. His arms are like an athlete's legs, brown and limber, and immensely strong. Slow-moving and definite, he uses words carefully as if he's saving them, like coins in a piggy-bank, for a special occasion. During an average day he might speak, reluctantly, a dozen times.

His wife, Phyllis, big-boned and also very tall, has the same dif-fidence with language, and their bond has grown in their years of silence under Mt. Macedon.

Around noon, Norm has his head inside the hood of his Chevy truck and Phyll's watching him closely. There's a nut on the generator-bracket which, despite all his grunting and yanking, won't give. Suddenly the spanner slips and his arm slews, with immense force, across the fan-blade. Blood rushes out of his wrist. He says nothing, just tightens his jaw and keeps trying to free the nut, while the blood flows.

After a few moments Phyllis puts her head closer and says, very slowly, 'Don't get blood all over your engine, Norm.' Her tone implies that this is the most natural of concerns. Norm doesn't react to her or to the mess on the engine. He keeps grunting and wrestling with the nut.

*

At five o'clock with the shadow of Macedon falling across the sheep-pens, Norm's at the sheep-race, his wrist heavily ban-daged. He's trying to separate the two-tooth wethers from the rams and ewes and he makes a sound like '*Ho*' when one of them gets stuck in the gateway. It's all very routine, until one of them becomes firmly wedged and refuses to move. At this, Norm shouts 'Ho' then 'Ho' then 'Ho', quickly and loudly, a dozen times, his voice rising with each repetition. Then he stops. He leans back on the fence-rail and looks up at the depth of the evening sky and then begins, rather quietly at first, but with mounting intensity,

You up-strung dunny-rat piss-drinking son of a jacked off pig-fart, you cur-brained bum-headed dingo-rutting monkey-faced crotch cannibal, you offal slop, turd-choke bollock-bag slack-doodled derro-witted slime-sack, outta there you greasy toad-ball, sewer-swilling pin-peckered bastard GET outta there RIGHT NOW.

I'm almost fourteen and I'm convinced I know all the cuss-words in the language but this is new, this is really new, and Norm's wife and mother-in-law have heard it so rarely that they run onto the porch, and Phyll exclaims in a delighted loud whisper, 'Norm's swearing!' and the three of us listen while Norm's words rise into the still sky and seem to bounce off Hanging Rock. It must be a secret rite that he learned for special occasions from his father and his father's father, and now he takes a huge breath and resumes the performance with a full orchestral flourish:

You pig-rooting bugger-faced ball-squeezing son of a dingo-mongrel, I'm gonna pull your pizzle through your belly-bing-hole, I'm gonna splatter you with dunny-juice, break you in ficking half with the whacko pizzle of a bog-bull if you don't get outta there, get outta there or I'll push your doodle all the way into jacks-ie-country, all the way from wombat-hole to breakfast time.

GET OUTTA THERE!

Just as abruptly as he began, he stops. He goes back to the sheep-race and quietly says 'Ho', swings the gate once, and the stuck sheep frees itself, and makes its way to the right pen.

It's as if nothing at all has happened. The silence closes round us and Phyll and her mother go inside, their faces aflame with pleasure, and Norm keeps dividing the rams from the two-tooth wethers until they're all at home in their separate pens.

*

Next morning, just after breakfast, Norm stops the Chevy by a large tree that's growing too close to the track, and takes his axe from behind the seat. He rubs his thumb carefully down the blade, peers along its edge, then begins. His swing is firm, unhurried, rhythmical.

At first I don't notice anything. The trunk seems to remain intact in spite of Norm's attack. Just as I'm wondering about his technique, huge wood-wedges start to fly out of the trunk and in a few seconds the tree crashes over, away from the track, exactly where he'd planned.

That night after supper, in moonlight so dense you can almost drink it, I stroll along the track and peer at the stump. Norm's cut is continuous, as if made by the keenest of saws, but smooth like the surface of a well-polished table.

I look very closely. Neither on the stump nor on the bole which he brought to ground can I discern the faintest markings of an axe.

*

Norm's two dogs are huge and mean and they scare the hell out of me. At knock-off time he asks me to feed them the swill from a huge rusty basin. The dogs are on chains designed so that they can't get to each other. They have cast-iron feeding-pots and there's a space of about two metres between them. I approach the pots very gingerly watching for any movement. The dogs are electrically alert and, fire in their eyes, they follow my every move. I pour the slop in their pots and move back and as I do they leap at each other so fast that I tumble backwards trying to get away. Someone's made a mistake: the chains are too long and the dogs can easily attack each other.

Then everything happens so quickly my eyes can't take it in. There's a whirl of snapping jaws and snarls and the air becomes a blur of torn hides and fur. All I can do is stand back and watch, horrified by the carnage. Norm comes running through the gate very agitated, yelling *'Don't let them fight, son!'* With that he picks up one of their huge saucepans and begins wielding it like a mad batsman right at their heads and after a while he makes enough contacts to slow them down just a little, but it takes some time to make them stop completely and by then the ground's flecked with rags of bloody fur and bits of ear. In a few seconds Norm's in command and, still wielding the saucepan, he gets them to back off, and shortens their chains to where they should have been. 'These are good dogs' explains Norm, 'gotta be protected.' His words don't square with what I've seen. The two half-ruined creatures flop down at the ends of their chains, bleeding profusely and still snarling, the fire in their eyes unquenched. Norm walks toward them waving the saucepan. 'Now lie down you buggers—and or I'll break your scones.' As we walk back to the house I figure he must keep the dogs on the farm for some reason, which I never discover.

CHRISTOPHER JOHN, MY FATHER'S FATHER, has adored his wife, Lillian Caroline, for many years, and she him. You can tell by the way they follow each other with their eyes, then pretend they're looking elsewhere. Their affection runs like a strong river in this large weather-board house, with its central hall-way that gives onto bed-room after bed-room and onto the airy living-room with its loud mantel clock and fire-place, around which the whole family—three generations—gathers on Sunday evenings.

Neither Christopher John nor Lillian Caroline speaks much. They move about their days and their chores slowly, but never sluggishly. The idea is to keep things steady. They are the root of this house and this family. No need for hurrying.

Everyone's welcome here: aunts, cousins, relatives from the mainland, farmers and fishermen, uncles with their stinking pipes and stories, the grandchildren and my school-pals from Melbourne, the silky-terrier, the cats and the backyard chooks and geese. This is a serious house; when you step across the threshold into this calm river, you sense instinctively that there are subtle demands. Here you do not raise your voice. Essential courtesy is required, even of the smallest children.

*

Grandpa keeps an old Essex tourer in the garage. It smells of dust and dry leather. The battery's dead but David and I take turns behind the wheel, adjusting the old choke lever and throt-tle and ramming the car into gear. The stationary car with its green duco and off-centre dials will always be roaring in my mind.

One day we ask Grandpa to take us for a drive and, to our de-light, he charges the battery, sets us in the back seat, cranks the handle and we're off around Devonport, down to the Mersey, past the breakwater where he sometimes catches a black-back salmon or a pike, then round to the Bluff where we take a quick swim, then back home via the Firth of the Forth. With the wind raking our hair and the car purring along and Grandpa, huge and eternal, behind the wheel, we want this day to go on and on forever.

Next day out on the garden deck Aunt Madge, Grandpa's daughter, joins us under the green-gage tree with its swollen fruit hanging like globes above us, and she tells us a story:

'Dad used to work on the wharves, you know. Difficult job, especially in summer. Well, one day it's brutally hot and he works so hard that he decides to call into the pub on the way home to wet his whistle. He almost never does that, but he does this time, and he gets home a bit later than usual to find the food on his plate almost cold. When he leans over to kiss Mother and she smells his beer-breath she turns away and scowls at him. Dad doesn't say a word, just goes outside to cut some wood for the kitchen stove, and he takes his time. When he comes back Mother's still pouting and showing him her back. He still doesn't say anything—just walks over and hoists her up, very gently, onto his shoulder and carries her along the hallway to the bedroom, Mother kicking the air all the time, and spluttering. I'd gone into my bedroom, which is opposite theirs and I could hear everything.

'So there they are in the bedroom, and what does he do next? He lifts her off his shoulder, high toward the ceiling and sits her on the big black wardrobe he'd made years ago for their wedding. Mother doesn't like this at all and she hammers the wardrobe with her heels. Once again, Dad takes no notice. He saunters down the hallway, works on stacking the wood-pile and returns to where Mother, who's really furious now, is drumming her heels like mad against the wardrobe. Dad turns and goes outside again, adds a few more pieces to the pile and this time when he comes back, the drumming's stopped and Grandma's sitting quite still. I could see all this through the key-hole in my door. He looks up at her and smiles, and she tries really hard not to smile back but doesn't quite succeed—so he reaches up as she reaches down and there they are standing on the floor, her head no higher than his breast-bone and he leans over and whispers "All right, Lil?" and she says "All right", and they both go back to the kitchen and have their tea.'

Aunt Madge smiles as she remembers all this, then continues:

'About that time, or a bit before, Dad takes up boxing. You know how big he is, but brawn and power don't interest him at all. It's the footwork—the feinting and the guessing—that's what he likes. There's also the rules. He knows that slugging's a part of the game but he thinks of himself as a craftsman, not a bruiser.

'But, I tell you, some of his opponents thinks that's all nonsense. They come out hard, fists flailing every which way, and if they accidentally catch you too low or knock your ear away from its root, it's too bad, mister.

'One time, at the height of his skill, he has to fight one of these fellas and when he steps into the ring he knows he'll have to be quick and clever because this one, by the name of Gillespie, is a brute of a man, a terrible bully. Dad's seen him knock the stuffing out of one of his own mates on the wharf for no reason at all, and he doesn't like him.

'Well, for a while Dad keeps Gillespie guessing with clever boxing and an occasional clip on the chin, which is his specialty—and Gillespie's getting more and more impatient because he can't find an opening for his knockout punch. Dad keeps clipping away and dancing around the ring and he lands one beauty on the solar plexus, which pulls Gillespie up solid. And now Gillespie's mad and, breaking all the rules, he barges in, fists flying, and one of his round-arms catches Dad in the groin.

Dad's in real pain, but Gillespie's so clumsy that he's spun himself onto the floor and Dad has a few seconds to lean on the ropes and catch his breath.

'When Gillespie gets up Dad begins to teach him a lesson. He's not trying to knock him out. He's boxing, scoring points. He clips him and clips him and then lands another one, hard and fair, in his middle. This time Gillespie's so furious that he stops dead. He looks at Dad, hating him. Then he sucks his mouth full of blood and phlegm, jumps forward, and spits it all over Dad's face and chest. For Dad, this is a vile thing to do and he's had enough. He steps in and, with one huge round-arm, knocks Gillespie flat. He leans back against the ropes while Gillespie writhes on the floor. Then he walks over and lifts him to his feet and says, "Sorry, Tom, but you made me mad—and you know why."

'Then he does an unusual thing. He undoes one of his gloves with his teeth, then the other, and flings them both as far as he can out of the ring. Then climbs through the ropes and, blazing with anger, stalks home.

'From that time on, Dad never put on a boxing-glove. Not once. Mother said it was because Dad had broken his rule: *A man has no business in a boxing-ring when he's full of anger.*'

EACH AFTERNOON WHEN BRIAN AND I get off the tram and make our way down Austin Street towards home there's something we have to do. We're forced to the edge of the pavement where we have to lean over at such an angle it's very difficult to walk. Someone's lifted up ten yards of a falling fence and attached it loosely with a piece of wire to a nail-hook on the last post. The road's narrow at that point and we know that if a car rounds the corner very fast it will take us with it. So we have to hold close to the pavement, as we lean. We must have done this a hundred times.

One afternoon Brian decides to do something different. This time, as we make our way awkwardly under the fence, he doesn't say anything but when we get to the end, he props his shoulder against the wood and quickly flicks the rope off its nail-hook.

Then he sprints downhill, very fast. I only have time to get out of the way as the whole fence crashes down and sprays broken palings out into the road. By that time Brian, who in his final year at school will run the 100 on a grass track in 10.4 seconds, is way down the hill, and making for the driveway of his home. I chase after him, hoping that the people in the house we're running from won't assume it was my fault that their fence has crashed over, while Brian gets off scot-free.

The next morning we walk past the gap where the fence used to be. I don't say anything but I notice that, though Brian's also mum, there's the flicker of a smile playing round his mouth.

RON AND I HAVE BEEN READING Hopkins and Milton and discussing religion on the cool green lawns that surround the University Union. Now the holidays have come and it's time to earn some pocket-money for next term. We apply to William Angliss' meat-processing plant, are accepted, and next day we find ourselves wading in big boots through foul fluids on the killing-floor which steadily rise as slaughtered animals, hanging from slowly moving chains, are hacked to pieces.

Ron's job is to poke about in the mess and separate the lower intestines from the heart, lungs and liver. They give him a long metal stick with a hook on the end and show him how to pull the organs apart, all of them still steaming, and then slide them along on separate paths to gaping holes on the killing-floor.

My work's even simpler. I have to collect all the lopped cattle-hooves and place them in a little barrow, wheel them over to another hole in the floor, and tip them down. After a while there's so much mess on the floor—an ankle-deep slush of blood and piss and bile and offal—it's difficult to see the holes, and the floor's treacherously slippery. One of the butchers bends down and whispers in my ear 'You have to watch yer feet, son. If you slip down the hole you'll be glue in no time.' He laughs maniacally.

Suddenly above the hum of conveyor belts and the noise of a hundred butchers at work, there's a high-pitched yell and all the machines stop. Everyone runs to the well where they winch the slaughtered animals up on chains. Apparently they've got an animal down on the killing-ramp that refuses to die. Generally, an animal will drop after the first or second stroke of the sledge-hammer at the base of the skull. We look down the well and someone yells '*Nine times! Jesus, that's a record.*' We're just in time to see him struck once more, and he crashes over. Everyone cheers, apparently for the beast, but we're not sure. The machine kicks into action again and quickly they put chains round his hooves—the ones I'll have to gather and dump in my trolley. Then they haul the beast up the well-shaft, hack off his head, cut out his tongue and add him to the belt of hanging beasts that, for a hundred yards or so, circle the killing-floor.

At knock-off time we go downstairs into the dressing-room and change out of our sodden boots and pants. The inescapable smells almost make us gag. A couple of the skilled butchers are there, already dressed to leave. You know they belong among the skilled workers because they wear special black pin-stripe suits—vulgar but expensive. They don't speak to each other. As they pass us on the way out to the pub we note that their eyes are hard, black and very cold. They look at us out of a vast emptiness. It seems that something behind them died a very long time ago.

The author (left) and Brian Austen, ca. 1950

IT SEEMS THE WAR'S COME BACK. The radio tells us, over and over, the whole country's in flames. Pools of tar bubble and boil on the roads. Hundreds of old people are dropping dead in the streets and in their houses.

Brian and I have decided to hitch-hike north, 1000 miles. We're freshmen and the world's our oyster. Our destination's a town called One Tree in southern Queensland. We want to see if it really exists, and if there's only one tree there. Temperature in Melbourne: 114. The radio tells us the huge sandstone chapel at the University is now a black ruin, and we're heading north toward the Equator, to the world's hottest zone. We realize there's something really out of whack with the world, and with us, but we keep heading north, north.

On the third night we camp at the Hunter River, usually a sizeable stream, but here today it's no wider than a garden path. The leech-infested pools hold water that's a little cooler than the air around us, so we squat in it until midnight, plucking off the leeches, chatting a bit and gazing at the moon. Even the moon's on fire; it seems to be mocking us.

Naked in our hammocks we still can't sleep. By six a.m. it's already 103, so we hurry onto the highway before the real heat begins and hitch a ride to a tiny country pub, the only building for miles in the smoke- and heat-haze. We lunge inside out of the glare and the heat which rises from the earth in waves.

On the bar two watermelons in a box—huge and dark green, with beads of ice-water wobbling down their skins. They're the only cold things in the world, and we want them. The pub-own-er, a taciturn bloke, reads our thoughts: 'No, no—not them ones, boys', he says. 'A bit outta your price-range.' He must have guessed what was in our wallets. So we sit in the dark and drink water warm as our arm-pits—glass after glass of warm water.

Soon, a huge truck with a huge driver in a blue singlet pulls up. He downs three cold beers very fast, while we watch him, hating him. Then he turns and says 'I'm headin north, boys. Wanna ride?'

Outside in the blinding light he tells us what we don't want to hear: 'Have to squat on the wheat-bags on the back, I'm 'fraid. Use yer army hats for the sun. Yous'll be alright.'

Then he makes a mistake: he leans his arm on the window frame of the truck-door. Immediately, the over-heated metal grabs his skin and in less than a second his arm's soldered fast to the door-frame. He gives out a hissing '*Jesus! J-E-E-E-E-S-U-S!*' Then he begins screaming, his free hand banging the truck door again, and again. The pub-owner and his mates run out and one of them pours a bucket of water over the truckie's arm and the door-frame but nothing can stop the screaming. The blood under the skin of his arm must have been, literally, boiling. Someone shouts: '*Let's get a fucking ambulance!*' while we stand there staring, horrified and helpless. The pub-owner walks over to us and says, very quietly: 'All right, boys. Let's get inside', as we try to shut off the truckie's animal screaming.

In the dark of the pub, without a word, the pub-owner rolls the two big watermelons out of their box and onto the bar, and cuts them through. He gives us a half each, takes one for himself and, still not speaking, lays spoons beside them, and a big metal bucket.

When you mush up the flesh of a watermelon in your mouth and swallow all the juice, then blow all the pips out and rattle them, like tiny machine-gun bullets against the sides of a metal bucket it's one of the purest pleasures. We're experts at that, and we sit and gorge ourselves until all the pink flesh of our melons turns white. Then Brian, quite suddenly, lifts up his empty gourd and pulls it down right over his head, and I do the same. It's cool and sweet-smelling in there and though we can still hear the truckie's screams they're much fainter. We want to keep our heads inside our green helmets but it's finally a matter of honour: we have to take them off. We have to endure the horror the truckie's going through, and his screams. It's only fair.

In a few minutes an ambulance slews to a stop in the graveled yard.

When it finally drives away we can hear the truckie, still screaming.

GRANDPA'S DYING AND THERE'S NOTHING we can do. When I think of him the form is of a slow-moving tower. He has to bend his head to get through the hall doorway. A giant of a man but quiet as a wheat-field. This morning he dragged himself in pain out of bed and passed me on his way to the lavatory, where I was whittling a model airplane by the tank-stand. I greeted him as cheerfully as I could:

—How's it going, Grandpa?
—Not so good, son.

I felt useless, and alone, and kept whittling against the nothing inside and around me.

On working-days Grandpa comes home for lunch at twelve precisely, then stretches out on the couch, and the silk-terrier lies on his chest and will not move until, at one exactly — you can set your watch by it — Grandpa rises and goes back to work. For the terrier, and the rest of us, this one man defines the world we live in, but he exercises no obvious authority other than his kindness. I have never heard him raise his voice.

Now the tower's cracking. There's no sound, only a crumbling from within. Wherever we are we all hear it. We move about, heads down, as if treading on thin glass, trying to stop it happening but we have no power against it.

*

They've sent me across the river to East Devonport to stay at Wilmot Winspear's farm, with its huge kitchen and a window that gives onto the pebbled shore of Bass Strait.

Wilmot tells me there's a creek to the west of his farm that runs down to the sea and it's crammed with tiny mountain-trout. 'All you need is a bent pin and a few bits of worm. Give it a go', he says.

I cut myself a rod, find an old length of fish-line and set off for the creek. All the way down to the shore I can hear the whoosh and boom of the surf. The day's brassy and warm; it vibrates like a struck gong, but where the little creek bubbles over its pebbles before it dashes into the sea, it enters a kind of cavern of thick-leaved bushes and there, on the cavern's edge, in the half-dark I stick my worm-bit on the tiny pin-hook and flick it into the water. The response is immediate: a fierce fingerling, no more than two inches, grabs it in his teeth and is off. I jerk him out and flick him into the old metal bucket where he flaps about, banging the sides. I dip the bucket slowly in the water and the tone of his desperation changes to a watery twitching.

Soon I'm hauling out more fish than I can count. After an hour or so I stop, thrilled and exhausted. We'll have a nice little feed for supper. You heat the oil in the pan and throw them in, for about ten seconds. Then you scoop them out and eat them whole—bones and all—with slabs of buttered bread. The taste is unforgettable.

As I'm thinking about this I notice something strange in the water. In the shadows, for a moment, a large head rises quietly to the surface and sinks back into the water-gloom. I look closely, and there it is again. What's that? It seems too huge for this little creek.

I have an idea. What if I take one of the tiny trout from my bucket and cut it up for bait? Maybe the trout won't eat their brothers but this big fish is definitely no relation. I move forward quietly, then drop the baited hook in the spot where I saw the giant head disappear and for a full minute nothing happens and I decide to pull it out and go back to the fishing that I know. Before I can, there's a huge pull on the line and it goes taut as a fence-wire in my fist. I only have time to wrap it once around my hand before I plunge into the creek as it tries to pull me downstream and I stumble around in the creek, terrified, trying to get a footing among the rocks and roots and all the time this straining of the line around my hand. *He's trying to pull me into the sea!* Then I'm standing firm and beginning to haul him in and as I drag him to the surface I see that it's a very large eel, or is it a black snake, writhing there, kicking the surface with his tail as I stumble up out of the creek to a flat rock in the sun and now the eel has wound himself around the line and is trying to pull the hook out of his mouth by stretching the line with his tail and I can feel his electric intelligence and energy all along the line as I swing him up and crack his head against the flat rock and he keeps twitching and pulling as I keep on banging and banging him down, and now I'm really scared. At about the tenth blow he goes slack and stretches out on the rock, quivers once or twice along his whole length, and is suddenly still. A few flies explore his glossy skin. He's about twice as long as my arm.

I notice that my heart's almost jumping out of my chest but decide to continue fishing and this time I don't have to wait for more than a few seconds before the next one tries to complete what his brother failed to do. But no eel's going to drown me today even though this one's much bigger, and he really means it. Now I know what to do, and soon there are two eels stretched out on the rock like fat black belts drying in the sun.

Back at the farm Wilmot shows me how to skin them by cutting their heads off. Then you drive a nail through the peeled flesh into a fence-post and, with a bit of newspaper, drag the skin off like a sock. Wilmot goes inside and for a moment, even though there's no hair on my chin, I'm tasting my young manhood. It's been growing in me fast since my first plunge into the creek and, standing here with the knife in my hand, I feel my life in me like a strong tree. And I realize that, from now on, wherever I go I will have to live by ingenuity and silence.

I've almost finished skinning the eels when Wilmot comes out to tell me that Grandpa has died. I look into his eyes for an explanation, but none comes and I can't think of anything to say. As I'm putting the eels in a hessian bag a wet wind scuffs up from the sea and my hands go cold.

That night we cook the mountain trout in a large pan, then one of the eels and, in almost silence, we eat, while the late sun slants across the combers and the flat sea. Then we light the pressure-lamps and, each with his own thoughts, listen to their hissing.

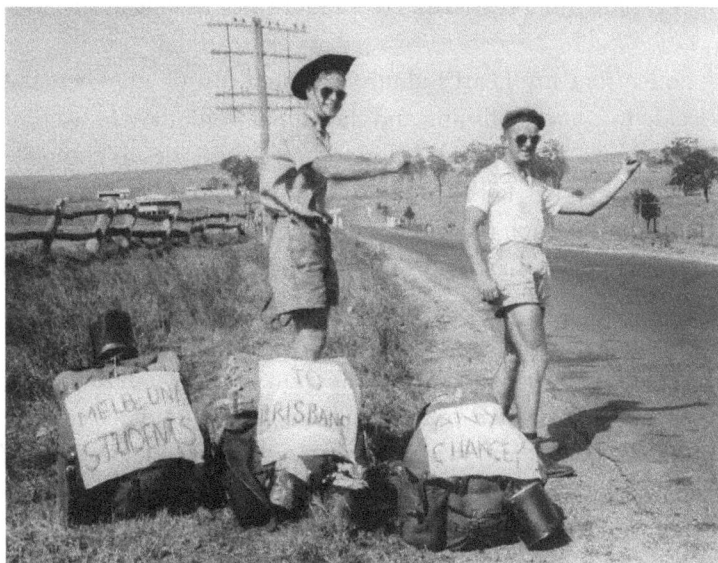

Brian Austen & K. h. ca. 1951

I HAVE JUST DISCOVERED Ezra Pound's translations in *Cathay* and it's as if some subtle elixir has entered the recesses of my inner ear and cleaned out all the rubbish. The whole book seizes my imagination but especially one little gem, supposedly scribbled on her fan by the wife of an ancient Chinese Emperor:

O fan of white silk
Clear as frost on the grass-blade,
You are also laid aside....

After that, there's no way out. You will have to deal with the fact that two *d's* can make a fan drop on a table and stay put, *laid aside*, like the Empress herself under her husband's indifference.

Something revolutionary has happened here. Pound has found a way to make the sounds of ordinary words release their energies.

WITH SOME POEMS IT'S NOT a question of learning them because you sense that you already know them. You simply forgot them this time around. Now, as you listen to the radio, this one's coming back and you recognize it immediately:

This ae nighte, this ae nighte,
Every nighte and alle,
Fire and sleet and candle-lighte,
And Christe receive thy saule.

When thou from hence away art past
Ever nighte and alle
To whinny-muir thou comest at last
And Christe receive thy saule.

The firm, largo movement of the poem, along with the masterful diction of the reader, draw me toward the words so that, as he continues, I feel I'm inside the poem, breathing with it:

If ever thou gavest hosen and shoon,
Every nighte and alle,
Sit thee down and put them on;
And Christe receive thy saule.

If hosen and shoon thou ne'er gav'st nane
Every nighte and alle,
The whinnes sall prick thee to the bare bane;
And Christe receive thy saule.

From Whinny-muir whence thou may'st pass,
Every nighte and alle,
To Brig o' Dread thou com'st at last;
And Christe receive thy saule.

From Brig o' Dread whence thou may'st pass,
Every nighte and alle,
To Purgatory fire thou com'st at last;
And Christe receive thy saule.

If ever thou gavest meat or drink,
Every nighte and alle,
The fire sall never make thee shrink;
And Christe receive thy saule.

If meat or drink thou ne'er gav'st nane,
Every nighte and alle,
The fire will burn thee to the bare bane;
And Christe receive thy saule.

This ae nighte, this ae nighte,
Every nighte and alle,
Fire and sleet and candle-lighte,
And Christe receive thy saule.

I can almost smell the soil in the fresh-dug grave over which I imagine the poem being intoned, and see the lantern being swung back and forth, back and forth in a compelling, hypnotic rhythm. I sit there on the edge of my bed, listening, wondering where such a fine thing could have come from and I'm grateful that, though the original singer and I are hundreds of years apart, we share the self-same world.

TALL AS A BELL-TOWER, very skinny and pallid, fresh from Cambridge, with a kind of detached look as if he belonged in another country and only doing this business of lecturing back here in Australia on sufferance, he reads Blake, haltingly, interrupting himself to explain a word or phrase, in a dry, barely audible voice. He turns to the poem called *London*, which I discovered only a few days ago, and which bowled me over. He reads it lifelessly, as if he were not really there. Unlike him, I've never been to London, but when I read the poem attentively I not only see the city, I can smell it and somehow get inside the minds of the people walking half-dead, down the grey streets, utterly alone. Blake's words tell me, unforgettably, how commerce has shrunk the Thames to a commodity, every inch of which is measured and given a price. Blake's view of the city is deeply sad and angry, and bald-head, the long one from Cambridge via Perth, reads on and on in his toneless voice and reduces the poem to nothing, and leaves us sitting there bewildered. Then he goes back and focuses on one stanza, and reads it, un-musically, again.

He pauses and, for the first time, looks up at us.

'That stanza', he allows, in his thin voice, 'is, I suppose, when you come to think, really not too bad.'

Enough, I say to myself, *this is not what I came here for*. I glance at my new friend, Max Kemp, who's equally angry and we both nod and rise. Then we walk out of the lecture-hall where the long one, the distinguished one from Cambridge, pretends not to notice as others join us. All of us are seething with one thought:

Sometimes you have to make a stand.

BEHIND HIS BACK WE CALL HIM Butcher. To-day, as he works on my mouth he's full of himself or of Moral Re-Armament, it's hard to tell. In any case, he's found a new belief that will transform the world. He tells me more about it while the anaesthetic takes and he pulls another of my teeth. Dr. Purdom doesn't believe in conservative dentistry. If a tooth shows the slightest hint of caries he has it out.

He persuades me to attend a meeting where people will be morally re-arming and talking about the loss of godliness in our age, and such, and I agree to go. When I get there I'm bored beyond imagining. This is not where I want to be. My eyes rove round the bookshelves in the suburban sitting-room and find nothing to hold them. Then I see a small, handsomely printed book on the coffee table. I open it, and read the first lines:

> *I do not know much about gods but I think that the river*
> *Is a strong, brown god—sullen, untamed and intractable...*

And, while all those around me are yabbering and making the world into a better place, nothing can stop me reading.

In the next few weeks I begin my long plunge into everything Eliot has written. His imagination is so musical and so accurate that he will hold me, sometimes against my strongest wishes, for many years:

> *The winter evening settles down*
> *With smell of steaks in passageways.*
> *Six'clock. The burn-out ends of smoky days.*
> *And now a gusty shower wraps*
> *The withered leaves about your feet*
> *And newspaper from vacant lots;*
> *The showers beat*
> *On broken blinds and chimney-pots,*
> *And at the corner of the street*
> *A lonely cab-horse steams and stamps.*
> *And then the lighting of the lamps...*

Has anyone written about the sordid, inescapable presence of the modern city with such pungency, and such authority?

Jenny Gibson in France, ca. 1957

OUR JOB, BEGINNING AT MIDNIGHT, is to sort the Christmas mail into correct piles so that the posties can pick them up in the early morning and carry them on their bikes all around the suburb.

It's obvious this skinny guy with his brown European suit and a flickering shyness in his smile doesn't yet belong here.

In fact, neither of us is suited for this job and we make lots of mistakes with the addresses on the letters, mistakes that sometimes come back and hit us hard next morning when a postie yells out '*What the fuck!*' and slams them down on the bench. Part of the trouble is that it's hard to stay awake all night, but when we can and when the supply of letters drops off we have a few minutes to chat and I find out that my new companion is called Richard. He's a violist and he's come to Australia from a Christian community in Palestine where his family were interned by the British during the War. After it was over they all came to Ferntree Gully where his father's started a farm. Richard's knowledge of music is amazing and he tells me about Hindemith and Wagner and I share what I've learned about Hopkins, A.D. Hope and some things I've been reading in the Vedanta.

We meet a few times after work and we both feel the power of a developing friendship. Then, as will happen, with the end of the Christmas season, our work stops and, as students will do, we go our separate ways.

Sun banging off the wall of the New Arts Building and a wind swinging every which way out of nowhere, whoofing down alleys between Quonset huts where students hurry between lectures. Loud gusts collide with our laughter and sweep our voices away to a far boundary so we only catch each others' words in short bursts.

At first I don't notice her, then do. I turn my eyes away; then look back. Something about her pleated skirt, about her yellow scarf and the way she carries it; something about the tone of her voice. It's very precise, yet gracious. Her whole presence is one of a simmering vivacity, barely held in.

Then everything dissolves in the wind and is carried off. Two weeks go by. Then she's there again, in rust and red colours now and we're free of the wind this time and I'm talking with her easily. It's as if we're caught in a music that we're also making. This is a new experience, and I want it to continue.

— 'WELL SHE MIGHT BE BEAUTIFUL,' Brian says, 'but the real question is whether she's right for you.'

— I don't really know what that means. Who's right for anyone else? All I know is that I can't stop carrying her round with me — not that I want to stop. It's strange, though. She seems to live in a different country and I don't have a passport and I'd like one. Is that what you mean?

— Something like that. Diane and I have only been together a few weeks and it feels like years. We seem to click and everything's going well. Touch wood. I can relax with her. I guess I'm lucky.

— Good for you. I can't relax anywhere. Anyway, Jenny's coming for a drive with me this Sunday. Can you and Diane join us? I think we'll go up into the hills.

— What, in that old wreck you bought last week? It hasn't even got hydraulic brakes. You reckon it'll get us out of town?

— It's not that old, and it's running pretty well.

— Okay, I'll talk to Diane, and if she's free we'll both start praying.

As we head back from Warburton I let Brian drive the Rugby. He's wearing a floppy old beach hat and Diane's head is almost completely hidden under a lairy orange beanie. Brian takes the wheel and when we get going he suddenly reaches over and swipes the beanie off Diane's head and puts it between his knees. Then he takes off his own hat, plonks it on her head and puts her beanie on his. They both laugh. They're already deep friends, and more. In a few months they will marry and to all who know them well nothing will seem more natural and inevitable. Their wedding, a few months later, celebrates a marriage that lasts sixty years until, one evening, Diane's heart stops.

Meanwhile, they make the world a gift of four strong daughters and their affection for each other never wavers.

Right now they're driving in my 1926 Rugby which is holding the road nicely and they're happy and I'm with Jenny in the back and the wind's tugging at our hats.

3
North:
London & Edinburgh

AFTER SEVERAL GLASSES OF SCOTCH, the vein in his forehead becomes a thick blue string that runs from his hair-line to a point just above his left eye, pulsing.

We're sliding, in evening light down the harbour, past the rising foundation of the Opera House then, shortly, out through the Heads and north to Singapore. I've spent three years in the prison of a country town and when, two days ago, the last streamer broke from the ship at the dock in Melbourne I experienced a surge of joy that was close to manic, and I fought to keep it down.

I strolled around the deck, listening to the wind-music in the ship's rigging. I tilted back by head and my whole being was singing:

I'm on my way!

Now we've formed a small circle in the forrard lounge of the *MS Skaubryn* en route to Southhampton—Jules who has just come from Brazil, and three others, and the talk ranges from politics to mediaeval history. Although we've, somewhat perfunctorily, introduced ourselves, we're still strangers and as I stand here listening I'm captivated by the cosmopolitan suavity and free-wheeling energy of the conversation.

A few days later one of Jules' friends sees me on the boat-deck and notices the book I'm reading.

— I knew I'd meet someone on this ship who likes Tolkien, he says.
— Well, I can't say I like it yet. I've only just started. Matter of fact, so far, it's not exactly my taste. I like my mythology straight.

He's only half-listening as he gazes out to sea and I notice the sharp blueness of his eyes, a sort of detachment that flickers somewhere between amusement and a certain cold calm.

He turns toward me.
— By the way, I'm Malcolm — Malcolm Calley.
— Yes, we met the other evening in the lounge.
— Of course — you're from Adelaide.
— Melbourne.
— Ah, yes.

I know he only half remembers me, so I give him my name again. He sits down besides me and we talk for an hour or so.

He tells me he will go to London to marry Laila, a Swedish archeologist whom he met in Bathurst a few months ago. They'll live in London while he does a post-doc. in Anthropogy at the London School of Economics. Malcolm's trim, his hair and his speech precisely clipped. He's thoroughly organized and seems to have the world just where he wants it. His doctoral thesis on a tribe in the North coast of N.S.W is being bound as we speak and everything about him seems cool, planned, immensely easy. Later we meet again in the bar and swap bawdy limericks. Many of his, he tells me, he's learned from Professor John Anderson and his cronies at the University of Sydney. As the ship knives through the flat Pacific along the East coast and across to Bombay in the next few weeks we get to know each other. I have no inkling that this friendship will be a central part of my destiny, or that meeting Malcolm will radically change my life.

Paul Ritchie, London, ca. 1980

AFTER A FEW DAYS IN London I take the cross-channel ferry and the train to Paris, where I've planned to meet Jenny at a café she found in her last visit to Paris from Annecy in the Alps.

On the way there, trying to negotiate the Metro for the first time, I make a mistake and hand my ticket to the clerk at the top of the escalator, who promptly punches it so that when I arrive at the platform the ticket-checker tells me I've already used it. I protest in the best French I can muster, but to no effect. I take the escalator back to the ticket office, buy another, descend again and tell the same lady, again, that this is my first time in Paris and on the Metro, and that I'm not a free-rider. I add that this is not the way to greet visitors from Australia. Australians, after all, fought alongside the French against the Germans. She stiffens her back, stands very tall and says *Je fais seulement mon devoir!* to which I reply *'Oui, et vous le faites fort bien!'* and hurry to hop on the train which has just roared into the platform.

The first thing I notice about Jenny is that she's firmly at home in France. In the café she speaks to the men and women with great ease. Her French is fluent and confident, mine stilted and uncertain.

Jenny's changed, and is very much the same. She tells me that in the south of France she had some periods of very disturbing darkness. None of that shows. We spend a pleasant few days in Paris, catching up, browsing book stalls on the Left Bank, then we both return separately to London where she's visiting friends and family and I'm settling into my new digs.

We meet a few times in the city in the next two weeks, then when she sets sail for Australia I find myself alone, back in my bed-sitter near the market in Ladbroke Grove. It's primitive, poorly furnished, with a colourless green patch of lino over half the floor. But it's all mine.

Now I have no excuse, I have to get on with it. The solitude doesn't worry me. Everything's become an adventure. I snuff the London air and stroll around the city, feeling the pressure of its history, the way it absorbs newcomers so that all of us seem to be committed, in the long run, to minding our own business. The impersonality of London has its own tonality and right now it's just what I need. In Australia I'd saved for half a year's rent and food so I don't have to look immediately for a job. I begin to jot down fragments of poems that have been swirling in my head these last few months. For the most part they're awful, but from the scribbles I garner a few good lines and I begin, very slowly, to do what I came for.

He strides through the doorway, and stretches out his hand.

— Helluva room! I ought to know, it used to be mine. Hi!
Name's Paul Ritchie. I know yours. The old geezer downstairs told me.

— The old guy told me about you too, Paul. Good to meet you.
You're right — this is some room. But it will have to do.

— So you've come from Sydney.

— Melbourne. The boat sailed from Sydney.

— I was born in Sydney. Haven't been back for 15 years.

— Where's your home now?

— Spain. Island called Ibiza. I like it there, but I ran out of cash
so I've taken a job in a Reform School near Oxford. Kind of
prison for youngsters. They'll probably kill me.

— What kept you away all this time?

— Good question. I love the bush but I can't stand suburbia,
and Australia's one big suburbia — English suburbia. Check
the names. All second-hand English. Australia's a kind of
cloud-cuckoo-land. I find it hard to breathe there. (pause) I
heard you write poems. Why don't you read me one.

— Okay. Here's something I've just been working on. Not quite
sure where it's going.

I read from the rough notes of a poem I'd jotted down earlier
that morning, and wait. He looks directly at me. I seem to have
met him somewhere before. He's quiet, thinking, then says:

— Bit pretentious. Sounds as if you're trying to write Important Literature. Not enough blood.

His remark stings, but that evening I look over my notes and see
that he's right and I'm angry with him, then with myself, then
glad of the critique. I have something to work on. I didn't know
what it was before.

Paul looks around the room. I have no idea what he's thinking.

— I'm off around the corner to meet some old friends in the
    Portobello Market. Why don't you come along?

We put on our coats and plunge out into the dank London air.
He seems to know every second person on the market-stalls.
Even though he's been in Spain for six months they greet him
as if he never left.

Paul has a satyr's face, a little like Jimmy Cagney's, young and
old, eyes crinkled at the corners, a mop of blonde hair. He
doesn't give a fig for any wisdom the world might have to offer.
Only people—the odder the better. And paintings. He shows
me some of his own drawings which the old geyser who owns
the rooming-house has been minding for him. A gallery of gro-
tesques, all of them intensely alive. The pen-strokes are electric.

Next day at the National Gallery Paul tugs my sleeve.

— Have a look at this Grünewald.

He puts his face almost against the painting. A guard stirs. Paul ignores him and beckons me to join him, very close to the picture.

— The detail's terrific. The twigs on the end of the branches look like witches' nails. But there's something else you have to see while we're here.

He leads me to Botticelli's portrait of Mars and Venus, which, like millions of others, I'd half-noticed before, but never studied attentively.

— Look at Venus' face. She's like a cat after a huge bowl of cream — now look at Mars. The god of war, and he's completely zonked. She's finished him, and his great spear's lying limp beside him — and look at the satyrs crawling through his helm and laughing their heads off.

Paul stands in front of the painting shaking with mirth and the guard, who's followed us, approaches us, looking grim. One is not supposed to do that in front of Botticelli. But the painting's genuinely funny and soon several people have joined us in front of it, and we're all laughing. Now the guard's very confused. He's never had to tell people not to laugh before. Most people seem to understand.

While in the Gallery, taking our time, we look at de Hooch and Hieronymous Bosch and della Francesca, and I learn more about painting in a short space than I ever have before. Paul has a very fastidious eye, and he combines this with a rare lust for extravagant life. He's an unashamed apologist for artistic brio. Brio with exactitude.

Of all the artists I've met Paul has the surest instinct. He smells fakery a mile away. Yet when he does he's rarely unkind. He often laughs lustily at a bad painting because he's done so many himself and says he's in no position to judge. But, at the same time, he has little time for bad stuff pretending to be worthwhile, especially his own. Yet he believes we should have a tolerance for innocently bad paintings, not get upset about them. Laugh, and pass on to the good ones.

Paul Ritchie is a mix, and the mix makes sense.

Back in Ibiza he's on fire with American fiction. He writes to me about Faulkner and Styron. Then, when I join him on the island, he introduces me to a dozen painters, talks about their paintings as paintings and the painters as people. He never gets the two confused.

When I'm back in England he goes through a dark phase on the island. He can't paint and he can't write. I write him a poem because I like him and want to say something useful. I call my poem *The Fallow Season*, a season I already know well, and I show it to him when he comes back to London. He asks me to read it aloud, and I do:

These shadows moving over new-ploughed land
prefigure a meaning which we darkly guess.
Under our feet where once the tall crop waved
the earth lies bare save for these yellow stalks
protruding at odd angles from the furrows;
these, and a few wet leaves that flap and scurry
long the fitful wind, are the last signs
of the strong, swaying harvest; for
this is the quiet time, the fallow season.
Ignorant men who pass will nod their heads,
saying: That earth is sour—and turn away
because no lushness springs to gratify
the sense, and hold indoors, keeping a sullen
fire, inwardly cursing the unyielding weather.

And while the white rain beats across the hills
it's desolate enough. But you, who by
some shrewd perversity or courage, toughen
on disappointment, will come through this
to make again. This is the quiet time.
Put down your brushes and your words,
Breathe with the earth, draw strength from solitude.

Paul likes my little tribute and I'm surprised, and pleased. It's undeveloped, I know, but there's a taste in it, a tang that's all my own.

It feels like a beginning.

I DON'T REALLY KNOW WHAT I'm doing here at Birkbeck College and neither does my new friend John Hopkin, a Welshman with flaming hair and a wealth of stories and ribald jokes. I'm supposed to be doing an M.A. and writing a thesis about Edwin Muir but I don't have any ambition as an academic or a scholar. I really admire Muir's poems but as I write about them they become more remote than the Orkneys which is their home landscape. Whatever ambition I might have doesn't include academic teaching because, when I think hard about it, I really loathe the idea of climbing the ladder of Success. Hopkin, who shares my views on all this, also has some vague notion that an M.A. might be useful but we'd both be hard-pressed to say exactly how. He's trying to write plays and I'm trying to make poems. That's quite enough.

Late one afternoon, after a very bad lecture on Pope, which does nothing to make the poetry come alive, Hopkin turns to me:

— Let's get out of here. I know a Welsh pub on the Gray's Inn Road where they can really sing.

— Count me in.

We find the pub and walk into the common bar, which is relatively quiet and very dark. We squint hard. There must be a score of people there, mostly men. We order beers.

When they come I decide to take a risk.

I stand up and call out, rather loudly, over the hubbub:

— I've just come from Australia and I love *Cwm Rhondda*. Will you please sing it for me?

I half expect them to tell me to get lost.

Instead, with no hesitation, they all burst into singing, robustly, and accurately:

Guide me O thou Great Redeemer
Pilgrim through this barren land...

After a few seconds I realize that they're singing in four parts. I know the hymn well and particularly relish the point where the melodic line keeps on hitting the fifth and the basses rise to meet it on the fourth and the music hangs on a prolonged dominant seventh. They do it beautifully.

I'm bowled over with admiration and gratitude. It feels as if I we're all in a film, but there's no camera-man here. At the end, I clap vigorously and they acknowledge me and go on talking and drinking.

MALCOLM AND LAILA ARE SETTLED into their bed-sit in Turnham Green, and have about them the air of two people who are thoroughly married. Their flat becomes a hub for anthropologists and visiting Swedes, academics of all kinds, and the conversation jumps and dances and the cider and beer never stop flowing. One night a Fijian post-graduate tells a story about his direct experience with fire-walking in New Zealand which he says he can't reconcile with his innate skepticism about such things. Laila regales us with tales of her eccentric family in the north of Sweden and, in particular, an aunt who likes ski-ing in the nude on remote mountain slopes in Jöteheimen and occasionally has to seek refuge from an inquisitive helicopter. Laila is also an amazing cook and she introduces us, along with their new friend Lucky from Sri Lanka and Pat, Lucky's wife, to all kinds of dishes I've never experienced.

So this is London and it's where I want to be. In a matter of weeks I'm adopted into Malcolm's and Laila's burgeoning London circle. Malcolm likes tinkering with his Bradford van and he and Lucky pull the head off and give it a complete valve-job. For Malcolm this work seems as natural as breathing.

Malcolm Calley, ca. 1965

WHEN MALCOLM INTRODUCES ME TO Lex Banning I notice Lex has to pause quite often as he tells his stories in order to suck in his breath. Then he rasps it back into the air as it tries to choke off his words. The pausing sounds like an extended, throaty *A-A-ACH.*

— So, what do you think of your first English beer, Lex?

Lex has been spastic since birth but that's done nothing to quell his energy, nor his quick intelligence.

We're sitting outside on the porch of a London pub. At my question he thinks a moment.

— Well, it'd be all right if they only *A-A-ACH* put some *A-A-ACH* bloody alcohol in it!

LAILA, AND HER SISTER CHRISTINA, who's fresh from her studies at Lund in Sweden, both smoke pipes. Malcolm turns to me and explains that they've been doing that for years. We're at a party near Senate House thrown by some of Laila's new post-grad friends in the Institute of Archeology. The two sisters smoke elegantly. I find it hard not to watch them as they stuff tobacco into their pipes and light up with a kind of nonchalant ease. Both beautiful women, they join vigorously in the conversation and they have no difficulty with English, which I find remarkable, particularly in Christina's case. She's never been in an English-speaking country before.

MY SAVINGS RUN OUT much more quickly than I'd planned and I take a teaching post in an inner London school. After some miserable months of trying to teach young men and women apprentices, who don't want to be there, but suffer the school because the government gives them a day off from work, I head south to the sun where Paul makes his island home. He's beginning to write fiction now but he still paints. Every week or so, to earn pocket money, he'll take a fresh canvas to the beach where he sometimes persuades a businessman from Barcelona or Madrid to give him a few dollars for it. He uses the cash to buy appalling Spanish cigarettes which almost disintegrate as he takes a drag. He's learned to live on almost nothing and his cash lasts him a long while.

I arrive in Ibiza from London in bad spirits, which the marine light and warmth of the island can't dispel. One night, walking back to the finca in broad moonlight, I decide to confide in him. 'You know, I feel so depressed with everything these days that I've sometimes considered just walking out there into the black water.' Paul hesitates only a moment.

'Look', he says, 'I think that would be a damn good idea, You're a real misery lately. Why don't you just do it?'

He stops, and looks at me hard. 'Go on, do it!'

I'm so surprised that I break into laughter. By God, he means it! He's pricked the bubble of my self-serving melancholia, and it bursts in the moonlit air. We stand there, laughing, the light dancing on the roof of the sea.

*

Paul has the genuine range of Whitman. Nothing human is foreign to him. He sometimes relishes the disordered and the depraved a little too much, but never loses balance for long. He marries Diana and has a daughter who becomes my god-daughter and they live in turbulent affection for years in Ibiza, then London. His two novels make a sudden blaze, then the flames fall away. He takes these changes in fortune with equanimity and still finds time to explore the authentic writers and painters of his time, and he relishes a good quarrel. The quarrels have guts. They arise out of a mind that cares.

*

It is these instincts that remain with him until the day of his last conversation with Portia and Rebecca, our daughters, who have become fast friends and who also love him without reserve. After which, on the station of Clapham Common, he takes a long drag from a forbidden cigarette, and his heart explodes.

The funeral service, in one sense, is disgusting. I fly over from Minneapolis to read a eulogy, and just have time to finish it before, with phony politesse, the funeral director moves us on so that they can wheel in the next coffin at the appointed time, and slide it into the flames.

Lex and Malcolm are obsessed with Japanese swords and Lex, who's only been in London a short time, already has a small collection. At dinner, he wants to show all of them. Malcolm warns us they're very sharp.

Lex begins to pull them one at a time from a kind of thick hessian bag that he and Malcolm have lugged upstairs to my sitting-room. Lex doesn't seem to care in the least that his arms don't always do what he has in mind, so the naked swords wobble and flash dangerously in the small space between us. We have to dodge them as tactfully as we can while he introduces us to his new treasures, some of which, apparently, are very valuable.

Well-schooled in Elizabethan and Jacobean poetry, Lex is a wellspring of Shakespearean quotations and literary gossip and he'll be missed by his circle of admirers back in Sydney, but now he's settling down fast in London as if he were born here. A prodigious drinker, ten schooners of beer seem to make no difference to his mental clarity. He and Malcolm discuss the swords, and drink and tell bawdy limericks into the night.

THE GUESTS HAVE GONE FROM Malcolm's house in Abbey Road. The redolence of a fine curry dinner hangs in the air. All afternoon, in miserable London weather, Malcolm has been grinding the valves of his van, fitting a new gasket then screwing the head down. Now it's running like new, he tells me. He looks well-fed, flushed, and very pleased with himself. Laila goes to the kitchen to make coffee. *This is the time*, I say to myself.

Malcolm opens a bottle of Slippervitz and before he begins pouring I tell him that I'm going to marry his sister-in-law, Christina, he turns, and says, matter-of-factly, 'Then we should give Felix a call.'
— Who's Felix?
— She's a medico. You met her here the other night.
— Yes, I remember. But why should we ring Felix?
— She knows a good doctor who can help.

I'm so amazed I have to struggle to speak.

— Malcolm, did it occur to you that Christina doesn't need Felix's help? I mean, did you think of asking Christina about what she wants? For that matter, did you think of asking me?

Malcolm doesn't hear what I'm saying. He's looking for Felix's number in his address book.

Christina harrison. ca. 1965

'LISTEN,' GEORGE WIGHTMAN SAYS, 'this country's produced some of the greatest poets in the West, but I don't think there's ever been a time when a group of them have given a public reading. Think about that! Chaucer gave a reading to the court of Richard II, but that was centuries ago. I think we should do something for poets now.'

— What do you have in mind, George?

— The Edinburgh Festival. Let's go and talk to Lord Harewood. He's running the whole show this year and he might be interested. I'll call and make an appointment.

That afternoon we drive to Harewood's office and Harewood listens carefully to what we say.

— I agree with you. So how can I help?

— We're wondering about a poetry week at the Festival. We've formed a group called Poets in Public and we're asking George Macbeth to join us and come up with a plan.

— He runs the poetry program on the BBC, doesn't he?

— Yes, and he knows all the poets.

— What do you have in mind?

— We want to propose a program of five days, three poets on each, with a singer and some musicians. We could invite W. H. Auden, John Betjeman, R. S. Thomas, Hugh Mac-Diarmid, a few of the younger poets like Ted Hughes. Maybe an American or two.

— Sounds interesting but you've caught me on a bad day. Make a proposal and send it along — and don't forget the budget. I have some tough Scottish bean-counters watching my every move. They're really mean. Anyway, get back to me and I'll see what I can do.

In the next few days we work very hard, then send Harewood a detailed proposal.

Lord Harewood is amazingly efficient. In a few days we have a contract to put on a program of poetry and songs in the Freemason's Hall in Edinburgh.

This is a first for the Festival. Very quickly we have commitments from three younger poets. We've also written letters inviting Auden, John Betjeman, R. S. Thomas and ten other poets, one from America.

Very shortly after that I catch the train to Edinburgh to check out the hall, the sound-system, accommodation for the poets, design a printed program, and a host of other things. In another few days we have acceptances from all the poets we want, along with two musicians and a fine reader called Harvey Hall who'll read an assortment of poems as a kind of interlude between the featured poets.

We're set to go and, when the time comes, we're off to Edinburgh.

'I THINK THAT'S AUDEN', says George, 'down there on the tarmac — for god's sake, he's wearing slippers!'

Auden shuffles toward us through the thin Edinburgh rain in a shabby grey suit, his slippers flopping about at the end of his legs and I notice that his ankles are turned inward so the inside edges of the soles are worn down almost to the felt.

As he approaches us he holds his right arm straight out from the shoulder, 'How varray nice that you've come to meet me.'

The usual wait for luggage, and banter about the flight from Austria, during which I try to remind myself that this is the man who has written some of the best poems in the language and who was possibly composing new ones on the flight. In the car he looks weary and a little bored as he tells us 'Every time I come to Scotland, I try to meet the Scottish poets at Milne's Bar or the Abbotsford, and they're very polite, and very sloshed, and they talk the most wonderful gibberish. So I still haven't really met them. Perhaps this time.'

Back in the hotel I begin the interview I've arranged for the A.B.C. but the tape-recorder gives up half-way through, and when I tell Auden we have to go through it once more he says 'Oh, no, not again!'— but he's not nasty about it, only patiently professional.

The interview over, we show him to his room. He looks around, and says 'I might be American, but I do like a bath.' He pronounces the last word to echo the vowel in 'lass', and I wonder if that's American or a survivor from his own northern English.

He examines the question that evening at length over dinner, along with the Albigensian Heresy, Russian versification, the poetry of Andrei Voznesensky, the origin of the American expression 'a quarter of five' (which has him completely stumped), and the cultivation of broad beans. We've ordered a fine Pauillac with dinner and he discourses without pretension on clarets and burgundies, about which his knowledge is wide. His English is poised and surprising—colloquial and erudite by turns, impeccably phrased. He has a high, dry tone that seems to originate from a place just back of the uvula as he tells us that the personality of the poet is nothing to the point. What matters is the poem itself. 'It's *varray* important to keep in mind that a poem's a verbal contraption'. The metaphor disturbs me but I say nothing and watch, fascinated, as he flicks cigarette-ash all over the front of his suit as he talks and smokes and talks until, at the end of the evening, the cloth of his lapels and chest are dusted with ash.

'You know,' he says, after a long silence near the end of our dinner, 'the saddest thing I've had to do for years was two weeks ago when I flew to London and went straight to the BBC. They'd asked me to write an obituary for Eliot. They were varray kind and gave me a nice office and all that, but I hated it. I sat there all morning and ground it out, and all the time I was conscious of Eliot out there, still alive, and very ill. Hell, that was difficult. He was a friend. But it had to be done.'

WE'RE SITTING IN THE FESTIVAL CLUB tea-room at the back of Freemason's Hall after a hard day of rehearsing and arranging broadcasts with the BBC. I turn to Harvey Hall.

— You have a really good voice, Harvey, and when I heard you reading in London I wondered if you've ever come across *The Lyke-Wake Dirge*.

— I don't think so. How does it go?

I say the poem for him.

He listens very intently. It's as if his whole body is absorbing the poem as I say it. He pauses a moment.

— Hell's teeth, where can I get a copy of that?

I write the text for him on a page of my notebook, tear it out, and give it to him. He reads it over.

— That's magnificent. I really have to do it on Friday.

'WELL, WELL, AUDEN'S TAKEN OFF his slippers and put on his street shoes', George whispers to me as we all gather on the stage. We're testing the mike levels and listening to a selection of the poems the authors have chosen to try out for their readings. My aim as producer is to make all the performers feel comfortable in the hall and to persuade them to project their voices so we can hear every word from the back row. Auden doesn't say much while he awaits his turn. Then he shuffles up to the mike, gets the distance and the level exactly right, and begins to read. He continues for a pace and then pauses.

— Is that okay?

— It's fine. I wonder how you feel about slowing it down just a little in the last poem. It's all fine and clear.

Auden's quite comfortable with the suggestion and goes to the mike again, this time with an excerpt from his new book *About The House*.

I listen from the back of the hall with George Barker who will read on Thursday. When Auden finishes his rehearsal I say to Barker, 'Come with me up onto the stage, George. I want to introduce you to Auden.'

— Auden? I can't meet Auden!!

— Why not?

— Auden's a god!

— Nonsense. He's very easy to meet.

Barker turns away. He has no intention of meeting W. H. Auden. Ever.

WHILE TALKING TO TED HUGHES just before his readings the first thing I notice is how huge and solid he is. It's as if a piece of Yorkshire granite has been given a voice and that voice, as he says in one of his poems, is 'as deep as England.' I ask him if he will read *Sunstroke*, one of the many poems that impressed me in his new collection, *Hawk in the Rain*. He's very polite about it but says he won't be offering that one this afternoon.

I wish him well in his reading.

IT'S OUR FINAL REHEARSAL and everything's going well. I'm sitting on the front of the stage taking a small break when a man in a very dark suit approaches and says, quietly:

— I'm a musician and I've always wanted to work with poets. Any possibilities? I don't need to be paid.

— That's very generous of you, I say, but the program's all arranged now and we don't have any open slots. What's your name, by the way?

— Larry Adler.

I turn to George Wightman, who's sitting beside me.

— I think we can find a space for Larry Adler, don't you George?

— I think so.

Suddenly I have an idea and turn to Harvey Hall.

— Can you do the *Lyke-Wake Dirge* for us, Harvey?

— Sure.

— Okay. Larry, please have a listen to this.

By now Harvey's learned the poem by heart and he goes to the mike and performs it superbly well.

I turn to Larry.

— I'm not going to make any suggestions. Just see what happens.

They both go to the mike and after a few words to each other they give us a treat we'll never forget: two extraordinary talents working together spontaneously in a way which is very rare.

— I don't know about you, George. But I think this is what we came for.

I turn to Larry and Harvey.

— That was astonishing. I wonder if I can make one small suggestion? Ignore it if you don't like it.

— Go ahead.

— Okay, Larry, you remember the part where the poem says

From Brig o'Dread whence thou mayest pass
Every nighte and alle
To Purgatorie fire thou comes't at last
And Christ receive thy soule…?

— Yes, I remember it well.

— Good. Well, I was wondering if you might put a slow chromatic slide at that point, Larry, something to bring out the terrifying eeriness. Maybe Harvey might pause there too — but that's only a suggestion.

— Okay, let's give it a try.

They confer for a moment then do the poem again, with a lingering semi-tonal bridge at the point I suggested and the effect's so frightening it makes us all catch our breath. Adler, as I already knew many years ago, has the skill to make the harmonica say anything he wants.

— You two are amazing. Can you remember all that for tomorrow?

They both nod.

That night in their performance they remember meticulously. The audience gives them its complete attention and when they've finished, everyone sits a moment, very still.

Then they clap, long and hard.

AUDEN'S LEAVING THIS MORNING, flying back to Austria and he and George are talking animatedly in the lounge when I arrive, almost too late, to see him off. He's given a fine reading of recent work and he's had a splendid time, though he tells us he still hasn't met the Scottish poets. 'They were even more sloshed than last time', he says. Without hesitation, he remembers both our names as he says good-bye, and shuffles toward the plane, still in his slippers.

The poet may not be 'the bundle of nerves that sits down to breakfast', but somewhere in that crumpled suit, ambling toward the plane, is the mind that wrote *The Shield of Achilles*, and a hundred other things that really matter, and will go on mattering.

George is silent as we drive back to Edinburgh. It's the kind of silence that accompanies a growing friendship and doesn't need to be acknowledged. It simply floats there, above the engine-noise of the car.

As the first pre-dawnlight slides into the bedroom I'm suddenly awake, and I find myself sitting bolt upright and repeating what I heard a voice say, very distinctly, in my dream: *Lex is dead.* Where the hell did that voice come from? Lately, Lex has not been in my thoughts at all. I turn to rouse Christina and share what I just heard. It never occurs to me that I could be mistaken. Just as I reach across to touch Christina I have the good sense to hesitate. She is the last month of her pregnancy and needs her rest. I say nothing but, nerves jangling, get up and shuffle about the house.

The odd thing is that I haven't thought of Lex for several months. He's been back in Australia for some time and his very sad marriage is over. The last I heard he was living in Sydney in great agony. The spasticity in his neck impinges on a nerve so hard that even prodigiously large doses of morphine bring him no relief.

Suddenly I sense his death with such vividness that I'm at a loss. About two weeks later a mutual friend of Lex and Malcolm writes to Malcolm telling him that Lex died on a certain day, and he also mentions the time. I make some quick calculations and am pretty certain that, allowing for the time difference, it's the exact day and time I when I heard the voice in my sleep.

I tell Malcolm. He's hard-core about such things and takes little note of the details, but he does tell me that the same friend who wrote him mentioned that they found a note on Lex's desk with my name in it. It was apparently in the draft of a letter Lex was writing to the *Sydney Morning Herald* about a review Max Harris had written for the *Herald*. Harris' review was a response to a piece I'd written in the *Spectator*.

— What was that all about? Malcolm asks.

— Well, the *Spectator* asked me to review Patrick White's book of plays. I read the book and wrote the review and Max Harris objected to it, claiming that, as an expatriate, I had

no right to criticize Australia's greatest writer. My guess is
that Lex sharply disagreed with Harris and was writing to
defend not so much what I wrote but my right to say it. Anyway, apparently Lex couldn't gather sufficient strength and
left the letter unfinished on his desk and, soon after that, he
died.

When I tell him all that Malcolm stands bolt upright, raises his
glass, and shouts:

— Good old Lex!

There's no way to explain to Malcolm that he's somehow miss-
ing the point.

BECAUSE HER DAUGHTER.

She has flown in fast from the Baltic.

Because her daughter, Christina, will shortly give us all a child who has no name. I look down from the tall windows into the light London fog as she stands ram-rod straight beside the taxi, and I can already feel her power. She comes out of the north-ern ice and an old culture. As I stand greeting her in the dowdy London hallway with its cracked, red linoleum I'm certain I've known this woman many years.

THE DOCTOR AND THE NURSE-MIDWIFE in the birth ward at Cross Hospital are both Jamaican, and they're very jolly, a fact that's not lost on Christina though her mind, right now, is focused on a single question: can they please help get this child out of her and into the common air.

I step outside the ward and make for the loo and in the corridor bump in to my friend, Peter Porter, whose wife Jannice gave birth here to their second daughter yesterday. I tell him I'm waiting for what could possibly be my daughter and that I intend to stay there till she appears.

— Hell, I couldn't go through all that. That's women's business.
— I'm not sure I'll like it but I wouldn't miss it, and I know Christina wants me to be there.

'Well', says Peter, 'good luck.'

JUST AS CHRISTINA AND I are almost giving up, our child starts to fight her way out. She fights hard, and she takes her time, and with everyone helping, there she is at last, here among us. I keep out of the way as there's great confusion in the small ward, but both the medicos are calm and they go efficiently about their business until Katarina, as she will shortly be known, is a blood-flecked tiny body in the doctor's hands. Christina looks dazed and mightily relieved. She manages a wan smile. Once again, I'm amazed at the sheer guts of this woman, my wife. She has hardly complained for a second during the birth, which was apparently as straightforward as these things can get. That's to say, it was very painful.

She turns to me and asks, very slowly: Boy or girl?

In all the busyness I haven't been paying any attention to that. Now I notice the new one has striking red hair and that this is definitely a girl. I tell Christina, who looks up at me sleepily, and smiles.

'We'll out-number you now', she says.

AFTER ALL THE BUSYNESS OF Edinburgh we're relaxing in George Wightman's flat in Earl's Court.

— The Festival Office has just sent me a telegram, George says.

— Saying what?

— ***CONGRATULATIONS! 97% SEATS SOLD EDINBURGH READINGS.***

— Anything else?

— Yes. ***MARLENE DIETRICH: 96%.***

— Well, I guess you were right, George. After 600 years the poets have made it into the open.

— Seems so.

George doesn't say anything more but he's smiling broadly. He pours us both a double scotch and, as we sip them, he peers across the roofs into the grey London twilight, and keeps smiling.

DAVID WEVILL, A NEW FRIEND whose work I've come to admire, and his wife Assia and I, decide to eat Chinese at a place in the deep East End, one that they both know well. Assia, as I noticed when I first met her is, in George Bernard Shaw's phrase, 'outrageously beautiful'. She has a simmering energy, dark hair, and a magnetic presence. She catches everyone's eye no matter where she goes. David lives contentedly a little in her shadow.

David and I have been sharing manuscripts of our latest work. David's sinewy poems have warmth and depth. He's a man and a poet of genuine substance. Both he and Assia are fine company and full of good life. As they've lived in the East for some years, and as I've had little experience with chopsticks, when we sit down to eat I ask for advice. Assia smiles and looks directly into my eyes: 'Be hungry', she says.

It works.

A few weeks later, Martin Bell and I who've been drinking bad sherry for an hour or so before our fellow-writers arrive, find ourselves at the annual P.E.N. celebration for this year's anthology of poetry in which we both have poems. Impelled by the sherry we begin introducing ourselves to some of the luminaries there: Stephen Spender, Bonamy Dobrée, and others. Suddenly I turn, and there's Sylvia Plath. I introduce myself and ask if Ted's here as I want to tell him he'll have his check from Edinburgh very soon. Sylvia stiffens, gives me a look as cold and large as an Antarctic ice-shield, and turns on her heel.

But she apparently makes a mental note of me because late next morning when I'm visiting Assia and David for lunch Assia turns to me while David's out of the room and in her high-toned, dramatic way, says 'I believe you were at a party last night.' She pauses and puckers her mouth, 'and you were really enjoying yourself'. Her remark carries a submerged freight, and I'm puzzled. My brain does a kind of quick somersault as it will when one's a little hung-over. Then it lands square on its feet. I knew Assia and David had spent some days in Cornwall with Ted and Sylvia and I also knew how much they both admired Ted and his work. I don't mention that but simply ask. 'Did I say something to Sylvia?' Assia doesn't answer but rolls her eyes in an odd way and, after a pause says, 'Yes, I believe you paid her some attention.'

I'm stunned at this because I know that what she said isn't true, at least not in the sense she's implying. I wasn't in the least drawn to Sylvia Plath either before I met her, nor after. I stand for a moment wondering what to say. I sense we could be entering delicate territory.

When I'd first started talking to Assia, David was seeing off a guest downstairs and, as she could hear him coming back, Assia only has a chance to lean toward me and say in a quick half-whisper: 'Ted's leaving Sylvia...' then she cuts away. 'I'll talk to you shortly.'

A few days later it's official. Ted Hughes and Sylvia Plath have split, and Ted's gone off with Assia, initiating, among other things, one of the most written-about romantic episodes in recent English literary life. Much has been said about the suicides of both Sylvia Plath and Assia Wevill. Not much, however, has been written about the collateral damage, including the death of Shura, Assia's daughter with Ted, whom Assia, inexplicably and horribly, took with her when she died. Nor, on the positive side, has much been said about the surprising productivity of Hughes in his later years, the generosity he showed young writers, the impressive contribution he made for many years to English literary life, and his unforgettable reading voice.

Nor has it been emphasized that those gifts came at an enormous price.
When I think of Assia I remember her very distinctive eyes,

which were not perfectly matched: it was as if one of them, I forget which, held the tiniest sand-grains and when she looked at you her gaze transfixed you.

The deeper natures of most human beings are more volatile and elusive than we like to admit. For this reason, in spite of our habit of doing otherwise, no one should be too confident about telling the definitive truth about another person. We're all simply too un-readable. Yet some of the evidence about Assia indicates that she was, among other things, deeply uncertain about herself. Retrospection indicates that she was, in an odd way, also ambitious and, not being able to produce something from her own imagination except advertising copy, she perhaps needed to be around talent and fame. I don't know. For my own part, what I liked about Assia was her disarming ability to be ordinary and vulnerable, and her quick sense of humour. Talking with her was a delight.

What I also know about Assia Wevill is that she was the kind of woman who should make a prospective lover wary and perhaps think: *Oh yes, this woman is very beautiful, but she's almost certainly dangerous.* And he might add: *If I'm going to dine with her alone, I'd best use a long spoon. Otherwise, there's a good chance I'll be devoured.*

There's a great deal to consider here and it's not easy to reach any solid conclusion, except perhaps this: whatever complex emotions compelled the triune drama of Sylvia Plath, Assia Wevill and Ted Hughes it was not 'love' in any sense I prefer to use that word. It was something closer to an unstable compound of daemonic possession, with all that often goes with it: jealousy, rage, radical mood-swings, depression, destructiveness and perhaps derangement: the whole thing.

There's something else: the fourth person, so to speak, in that triangle, who was clearly the most innocent one, if that word applies, is another story altogether. Whatever kicked my old friend David Wevill so hard in the guts and sent him packing, deeply wounded, to a place far away from London, was almost unspeakable. In one sense the nexus of Plath, Hughes and Assia was one of pathos, and even bathos. It's the task of those of us left living in the aftermath of all that fury to tease out the genuine from the gossip and the sensationalism, and it's a task in which the biographers have helped us only marginally. It may well be that such a project's impossible and will never be completed.

One could write a great deal about all this, but I will only add that some of the entries Hughes gives us about Assia in *Birthday Letters,* and elsewhere, cannot be characterized as the testament of a man who loved her.

I can't say much about Sylvia Plath. Others can, and will. She certainly had an intense imagination and a lapidary skill with phrase and cadence, and her poem *Daddy* is an astonishing tour de force. Reading her work as a whole, though, I hunger for air. As in much of the so-called 'confessional' writing of Sexton, Lowell, Berryman and others, her world has a population of one. It's too crimped, self-absorbed, enclosed. I've argued with many people over this and have come to the conclusion that we all have temperamental preferences, and mine are for space, amplitude, intellectual variety and generosity of spirit. My poetic talismans are Chaucer, Browning, Robbie Burns, Frost, Heaney and a large handful of poets whose vision is, so to speak, horizontal and comprehensive. Plath's almost exclusive focus on the burning self prevents me from being part of her audience.

There's a corollary: at the height of Plath's fame, shortly after her death, there was a widespread fascination with suicide as a subject for art. That tendency, for a complex of reasons, hasn't notably decreased. It is, however, one that, for a number of reasons, I can't share.

4
Westward

FIVE SUITCASES, THREE BOXES and a new baby: George Wightman drives us all in his car to Victoria Station through thick London traffic and we barely make the boat-train to Dover in time. George hands us our last bag through the train window, and we have time for a ten second farewell hand-shake before the train jerks forward once, then again, and we're off on the first stage of our journey to America.

LATE AFTERNOON. WE'RE WALKING on the surface of Stockholm Harbour. I'm uneasy because we're carrying Katrina who's well-swaddled against the sub-zero cold, but I've never walked on water before, and I don't trust it. Right now our shoulders are almost brushing the hull of a huge merchant vessel that towers above us. I slide cautiously across the ice and lean against it; then I bang my fist on the hull and produce a hollow reverberation and Christina and I laugh. Katrina sleeps on in her mother's arms. I'm amazed at how quickly she's adapted to being here on earth with us. No matter where she is, save for a few noises when she's hungry, she seems at home.

*

After too much food at Christmas dinner we all go skating on the pond near the family house at Urshult. As soon as I step on the ice I know it was a mistake. Almost immediately I'm partly airborne, then I seem to hang for a tiny second, as people do in film-cartoons, before the frozen pond jumps up and smacks me with such force my whole body is stunned. I drag myself across the ice to the softer snow-edge of the pond and several members of Christina's family laughingly lever me to my feet. I'm not laughing. I've been thoroughly bashed. Next day one side of my bum is completely blue.

These Swedish ice- and snow-sports go against my grain.

*

The *S.S. Mattawunga*, which we board at Göteborg and which is taking us to Boston in the depth of winter, has a cargo of steel, a small crew and five passengers. Almost as soon as we leave the harbor we're nosing directly into an Atlantic ice-storm which increases in force over the next three days. One afternoon the captain invites me to the bridge, from where I watch the prow of our ship lunging into black-blue water then climbing huge sea-mountains. It does this over and over and I think of our heavy cargo and the depth of the Atlantic beneath us and the thin steel skin that's keeping everything afloat on these dark waters. I turn to the radio-operator. 'What's our position?' I ask, as if that knowledge will give me some re-assurance. 'Don't know', he says, 'I can't get no signals.' The boat continues its climbing and plunging.

Days. More days. Only Katrina can sleep. The rigging and decks are entirely encrusted with ice. The ship does have a working compass and we know the direction we're heading. That's all. Fact is, while the radio's not working, we're lost at sea. When we finally break out of the main fury of the storm we're sliding South, parallel to the coast of Labrador which we can barely discern. It must be ten miles away and through the fog and sea-mist we can pick out a coast road with its tiny black poles. The road's completely empty and it continues for miles, and hours. On this vast white shore there's no living thing.

Wind howls in the stays. If we should lose our footing as we make our way across the deck, then drop off the edge of the still-lunging ship we will be, very quickly, solid ice. Will we sink to the bottom of the Atlantic, or float like the small bits of pack-ice swirling past our sides?

*

I'm with the captain again as we round Cape Race and into the Bay of Maine and head west for Boston. There's a large chart on the captain's table, and every few seconds he twiddles the dial of the depth-finder.

— Shifting sand-shoals, he explains.

I watch the dial. Suddenly the ocean floor beneath us rises to within twenty fathoms of the keel. Then the indicator drops. Then rises again. Fifteen fathoms. The pupils in the captain's eyes are hard black beads as, face taut, he watches the dial. Then the depth plunges to 100 fathoms, then more.

— We're over, he says.

I point to the chart, where the Bay of Maine shows scores of tiny back crosses.
— What are those? I ask.
— Wrecks, he replies.

*

In Boston Harbour there's no let-up in the freeze. The waters of the Mystic River are black which, it occurs to me, might be the colour of absolute cold. Our parkas zipped up, the captain and I are leaning on the rail as we wait for the pilot-boat.

'When I made my first trip here thirty years ago', the captain says, 'I was standing like we are now as the pilot-boat drew alongside. Some of our crew were greeting old friends on the pilot: "Hi Hans, Hi Jimmy"— when there was a sudden swell and the pilot boat cracked hard against our side and the boat immediately broke in two. The whole thing must have taken about three seconds, then the pilot boat completely disappeared—not even a hat or a pack of cigarettes on the water. Nothing. We all stood there and couldn't believe it. The pilot boat, with all its crew, had sunk out of sight. It was like a mad dream.'
—So what did you do?
—I called and asked them to send another pilot-boat.

*

The platform of the Boston railways station is so long that, in the heavy fog, we can hardly make out where it ends, and our carriage is the very last one. We're late and have to hurry to get ourselves and all our luggage on board so we move ourselves fast, up and back along the platform ferrying our heavy bags in shifts, and finally climb on board just as the train, without warning, jumps, pulls forward and heads into the snows of the interior.

We try to find places for the luggage and ourselves. No one gives a hand. A sudden dark premonitory feeling suddenly knifes through and I find myself thinking: *It's going to be difficult to get used to this country.*

*

Two days later I plunge out of our new home, a Quonset hut on the banks of the Iowa River, into a landscape of snow-drifts so thick I can't see over them and I make my way cautiously on an ice-encrusted track through a deep snow-corridor. I head for the Humanities building, where I introduce myself. The secretaries are kind and amazingly efficient. They have everything prepared for my arrival, including the texts I'll be using, and all kinds of brochures.

— Your classes will be on Monday, Wednesday and Friday. Twenty-five students in each. The first class begins at 7.30, the second at 8.30.
— But I'm not usually up before 9.00.

The secretary smiles understandingly. 'We start early here in Iowa. You'll need to adjust your schedule.'

MINNESOTA. PELLETS OF HARD SNOW out of some arctic hell strafe the classroom window. The wind whumps against the walls and sends the snow in huge waves over us and over the prairies from the Yukon to Chicago, then half across the Atlantic. I turn to the students.

'I think it's about the figure', I tell the students, and they look puzzled. 'It doesn't matter what we know or how many ideas we have. As writers, what we're looking for is the figure — the one that expresses exactly what we mean — and it often comes as a special rhythm.'

What am I doing in these white wastes of the American Midwest with a piece of chalk and a blackboard? I'm paid to teach these young people writing, and today I'm feeling like an impostor because, although I believe that you can learn to be a writer I'm not at all sure you can *teach* someone else how to do it.

Nonetheless, I keep pushing against the rampart of their wintry indifference.

I give the students a handout which, late in my study last night, I was convinced would help them see what I mean about 'figures' and the very elusive notion of 'rhythm'.

— Some of you know music, so I've copied out a bit of Mozart for you. It's the opening of a piano concerto.

They stare at the sheet.

On my old tape-recorder I've copied a recording of the first few bars of score, and I play it.

— That all happened quickly so I'll play it again. I've marked the hand-out with two groups of three asterisks, and I want you to listen carefully this time and note what's happening at those points.

The students listen again.

— Well, what did you hear?

Silence, except for the snow-wind against the panes.

— OK let me hum it for you because I want you to notice the stresses.

The students laugh a little as, very inexpertly, I try to give them my version of Mozart.

— Did you hear the rhythm ?

1 2 *3* 4 // 1 2 *3* 4 // 1 2 *3* 4

1 *2* 3 4 // 1 *2* 3 4 // 1 *2* 3 4

Did you catch the shift? You might have seen the film called *Amadeus* which was about Mozart and about the fact that Salieri was jealous of Mozart, partly because he couldn't make rhythmic shifts like that. Has anyone here heard of Salieri? No? But you do know about Mozart and what you've just heard is one of the reasons why. It's the rhythm.

The students look mildly interested. I sense that they want to tell me that this is a writing class, and what's all this with ancient music, so I try another tack.

— Mozart's having fun—like you do when you free-dance, and change your timing.

They're not convinced so I decide to come back to words. I'm paid to teach them writing.

— Writers talk a lot about expressing themselves. Well, Mozart's not expressing himself. He's found a change of rhythmic figure that's *expressive*. Very different thing. He's thinking about the music, not himself. He's an imp, like Charlie Chaplin, or Coyote. In a way, what he's doing is quite impersonal.

I feel I'm losing them. I'm a stranger here and have the sense that I will never understand this phenomenon called America. What in hell can I say about Mozart, or writing or rhythm or anything else that might be useful out here on this mad prairie in a sub-zero storm, the wind getting stronger all the time? My house is in a little hollow out there, somewhere in the whirling whiteness, and all of us are far from home, whatever that means.

But I'm not giving up. One of the students in the class recently played Hotspur in a college production of Henry IV, and he captured the role really well.

— Wayne, you were Hotspur for several hours the other night. Tell us what you discovered about him?
— About Hotspur?

He thinks a moment.
— Well, I liked the way he kept getting at the king, and how he hates all that artsy-fartsy stuff.
— Good. Do you remember his reply to Glendower in the Mexican stand-off—the scene where Glendower goes on about poetry and how good he is at speaking it? Glendower says something like this:

I can speak English, lord, as well as you;
For I was train'd up in the English court;
Where, being but young, I framèd to the harp
Many an English ditty lovely well...
A virtue that was never seen in you.

— I think I can remember. Let's see. Yes, Hotspur goes:

Marry, and I am glad of it.
I had rather be a kitten and cry mew
Than one of your same-metre ballad-mongers.
I'd rather hear a brazen canstick turned
Or a dry wheel grate on the axle-tree,
And that would set my teeth nothing on edge,
Nothing so much as mincing poetry.
'Tis like the forced gait of a shuffling nag

We're all impressed with Wayne's performance.

— Any of you ever tried to write an insult?

Silence again.

— Well, it's very difficult. The writing usually comes out too hot, or too stilted. You want to be writers. Okay, let's look at how Shakespeare does an insult. If you understand this, I promise you, you'll immediately lose your innocence. If you don't want to do that you should leave the room right now.

They're not sure whether I'm having them on, but no one moves.

— You might think, from what Wayne just gave us, that Hotspur tells Glendower that he can take poetry and shove it, and you'd be right. But that's only the shadow of the game that Shakespeare's playing.

I get up suddenly and scrape a piece of chalk, a full yard, across the blackboard. I have practiced this one and, luckily, it does what I wanted. It squeaks horribly.

— That's what happens when you turn a brass candlestick, or a 'brazen canstick', on a lathe. Same thing if you don't grease an axle-tree — the hub where the spokes of a wooden wheel all come together. It **GRATES.** You're writers. Listen to that last line, do you hear the rhythm? Can you beat it out on your desk?

They all bang their desk-tops:

'Tis like the **FORCED GAIT** *of a* **SHUFFLING NAG.**

ONE , TWO // ONE, TWO. Dead rhythm.

— I'm telling you all because you want to be writers. Now, here's the point where you lose your innocence. I have to be square with you. As writers, all you will ever have are words, and words are made up of two things, vowels and consonants — arranged in the best order for each thing you want to say. Think about it. Here's Will Shakespeare creating a character called Hotspur, a man of action who hates poetry, and he's created him entirely out of vowels and consonants in iambic pentameters. Yes, he tells us that he hates poetry — but he tells us all that in some of the best lines in the play. Very smart move. Shakespeare has invented a medium which is completely transparent. And, if we don't get the joke it's even better. We can join the groundlings in the pit who are on Hostpur's side and say: *Yeah, I can't stand poetry either.* But if we do that, Shakespeare's made complete fools of us, and now you've lost your innocence, you can see why.

I can hear the question hanging in the air: *But what's all this mean?* and I try to answer it:

— Well, if you're a writer your job's really a kind of verbal engineering. What Wayne gave us just now is real writing. Shakespeare's manipulating us by manipulating his words, and we don't even know it.

I pause.

— What Shakespeare's doing is very good work if you can get it.

The wind's still whacking the panes and the long limbs of the bur oak in the quadrangle flex and whip against the storm. Whether the students have heard me over the madness of the weather I won't know for some time, maybe years, maybe never.

NEAR MIDNIGHT OUR NEW FRIEND Bob Tisdale quietly pushes the door open. He knows we've been waiting for him.

'Time to go', he says. 'I've already rung the hospital. They know we're on the way.'

Even in small country towns in America the birth wards in hospitals are glossy, streamlined, impersonal. They hoist Christina onto a space-age metal contraption and tell me to stand at the head of it with a swab, and wipe her brow from time to time. In more ways than one we're in a different country.

Dr. Rysgaard's words are few, clean and clear. I stand at the head of the bed doing what I'm told. When things begin to happen I watch the top of Dr. Rysgaard's head. He seems to be making a calculation. Something tells me there's a problem and that this will be a difficult birth. I can't see exactly what he's doing but he's taking his time to explore. I begin to worry. Suddenly Dr. Rysgaard looks up, not at me, but through me, and I sense that he's riffling, mentally, through his old notes from medical school. I only hope he can find the right page. In a few moments, it seems he does. He drops his head. This time he has a large pair of forceps in his hand and I try not to think what's happening to my wife and the child she's trying to bring into the world.

Everything comes together as the doctor leans back, then forward, and quite quickly, whatever that means in this weird time-zone, Rebecca is here among us and she's squealing like hell. Another girl, with hair almost the same colour as her sister's.

A FEW DAYS LATER Rebecca's propped up in in her pram and she won't take her eyes off me. I have the sense that we're communicating. There's an intimate recognition but no words pass between us. She seems to be harboring some wry joke that's all her own. Later on I say to Christina: 'I think this one's going to end up as a special kind of surgeon — the kind that does tiny operations on the eyes of insects. Or maybe she'll be a cellist — but I think her cello will be a very small one.'

I was quite wrong about both those things.

Britt Haglund & Rebecca. 1970

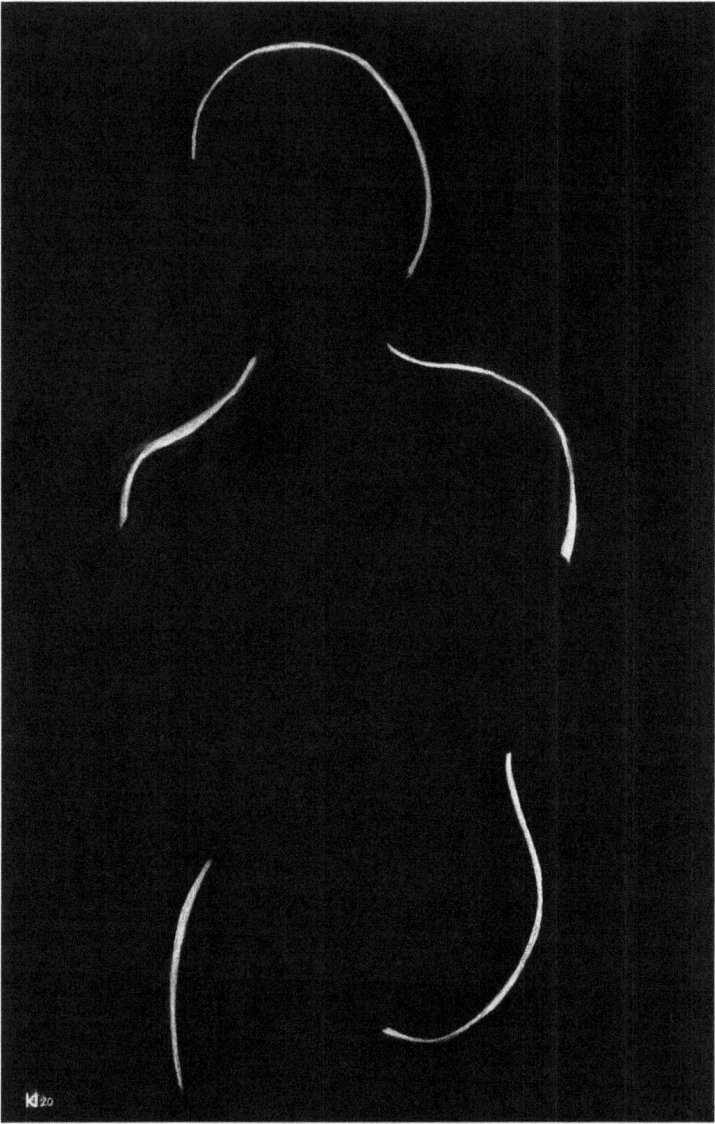

Christina, ca 1972

'This is it', I say. 'It's what we've been looking for. Five bedrooms—a huge one for us, one for the two girls, and a study for each of us—and look at the barn—it must be sixty feet tall!'

Christina doesn't say anything. She'd come to like the space of our airy upstairs flat closer to the town centre and having to leave it irks her. She felt at home living among the treetops. I relish the sense of being right on the ground, and the little creek that makes a tiny music as it winds among the black willows. The short cut through the woods to my office is also very pleasing. This is the first place where I've felt at home in this country.

Yet there will always be an uncertainty hovering round that feeling.

AS HE STEPS OFF THE KERB in front of the Union in the broad fall sunlight he looks distant and distracted. His suit is as dark as his face, and when I approach him to ask if all's going well for his visit I notice how ancient he looks. His name is A. K. Ramanujan, known to us all as Raman. As is sometimes the custom in Southern India, his name doesn't derive from his father, Atipat Asuri Krishnaswami but is a patronym bestowed on him by his father, in honour of probably the most brilliant mathematician in modern India, Srinivasa Ramanujan.

It's not an aging face, but the lineaments are old. They seem pure Dravidian. Right now, he's here, in America, enjoying his considerable success but he's also somewhat uneasy perhaps because everything's 'new' and provisional and experimental in this country, and nothing's clearly defined.

There's a restlessness in the air as the blood-coloured leaves twirl down, very quietly, from the maples, and Raman seems to be scowling. He returns my greeting, but his gaze is far-off, impassive. When I look, very quickly, into his face I have the sense that I'm being examined by the gaze of Kali.

We LUNGE INDOORS WITH BIG BAGS;
one splits and

bright cans bounce on our toes;
eggs by Jackson Pollock

wander over the floor.

We half-fall toward the table, laughing.
The big dog barks to see such fun.

This is my family,
their faces shining in the snowlight,

new snow melting in their hair.

Keith, Rebecca, Christina and Katrina harrison,
ca. 1972, near Loudun, France

'I COULDN'T HELP NOTICING', Raman says. 'When my son, Krishna, was four he kept jumping about the house, shouting "Big, fat hen! Big, fat hen!"'

The students laugh.

— I knew there must be some reason for it and I wanted to find out. I kept saying the poem aloud, over and over, and something began to dawn on me. Do you all know the poem? Good, let's say it aloud.

What follows is a ragged chorus, with variations on some lines:
One two,
Buckle my shoe,
Three four,
Close the door,
Five six,
Pick up sticks,
Seven eight,
Shut the gate,
Nine ten,
Big, fat hen.

— I know some of you prefer *'Shut the gate,'* not *'Close the gate'* — but ignore that for the moment. What did you notice about the whole figure of the poem?

They think hard but don't come up with anything.
He waits.
Still nothing.

— All right, let's say it again.
This time, at the end, they all declaim very loudly, **'Big, fat hen**, and laugh.

Raman's not in a hurry.

— Anything this time?

— The last line sounds very different.

— How?

— BIG FAT HEN. Three beats.

Yes. He strikes the table three times with his fist.

— So?

— The other lines go *Thump, Thump.* One, two. This one goes *Thump, Thump, Thump.*

— You're writers. What are we talking about?

— Beats.

— Any other words for it?

— Stress, rhythm.

— Good. We see it has a different rhythmic shape. So what?

Silence, but the silence is alive.

— I couldn't help noting the characters in the poem? Who are they?

— Shoes, door, sticks, gate.

— Then, in the last line?

They all shout the last line together
BIG   FAT   HEN

And, once again, the room rocks with mirth.

— Well?

— It's the only living thing in the poem.

— What else?

— One of the adjectives is unnecessary.

— Yes. Do you remember when you were a kid how you got enormous pleasure from repeating things? *My Dad's got a great, big, huge, humungous gun and he's gonna blow you away and blast you right up through the clouds and right into the sky?*

They're listening intently now as Raman leans forward:

— That ending was a real discovery for me as a writer because I began to think of all the poems I knew that did something different in the last line. You can probably think of scores of examples yourself. It's a sort of poetic stock-in-trade and it takes all kinds of forms. Sometimes it's a syntactic variation, or it can be a rhythmic change, or a surprising new image — or it can be a line much shorter or longer than the rest. But very often, as in *One two, buckle my shoe*, it's arresting because it's a number of things at once and we don't notice it consciously, but it's there, nonetheless, and it works. For fun, I called it the Big Fat Hen Principle.

The students are enjoying the class so much they forget they're in college. They're going on a journey which has barely begun. In the next few weeks Raman shows them how many ways you can look at the language in a poem. His thought ranges over the Bhagavad-Gita, Walt Whitman, nursery rhymes, folk-tales, Jewish mythology, the art of translation, the Indian gods, linguistic theory, and on and on, in such a liberating way that the students feel that, with work, they too can be authentic thinkers and writers. They realize that, beyond all the drabness and the bits of paper and the desks in serried rows, the mind can experience the dance of its own discoveries.

BRITT FLIES IN AGAIN, this time across the ice-cap, to our old farm-house to see her daughter and her new granddaughter, and she still has the same electric presence, omnivorous appetite for literature and languages, and what they call in her country an unquenchable *lust* for everything around her. She also has something very rare: a genuine taste for thinking things through. She's a committed follower of Rudolph Steiner and some of her ideas are pretty outré, but they are ideas, and what she says about the way kids develop, and how to best compost a vegetable garden, and much else, hold our attention. We have wonderful arguments.

But because she's so mercurial and impulsive, she makes mistakes. On the afternoon of her arrival, forgetting her age and her slightly calcifying bones, she takes Katrina's pony for a ride around the property and she's hardly mounted when the pony throws her off against a fence and she cracks two of her slightly calcifying ribs.

Christina's off each morning early, working on an archeological dig miles away, on the banks of the Mississippi. So, day after day, I bring Britt meals to a bed we've rigged up on the front porch, and one afternoon when I'm muttering *sotto voce* to a friend 'Silly old thing. Hardly gets off the plane when she wants to ride a stupid pony' she overhears me and tells me off with a wonderful scorching anger and I retreat to the kitchen, shame growing over me like hot leaves.

As she heals, she teaches the children a new kind of drawing, cooks pike with a flaming horse-radish sauce and introduces me to Mr. Johansson's Temptation, the taste of which is unforgettable. She gets on with life, right here and now, with that combination of focused practicality and a kind of dreamy 'scanning' found in people who are both physically and mentally evolved. She is a very beautiful woman and she makes all the difference. Then she flies back to her northern ice.

Some years on, in her tiny church in Helsinki, in the middle of her sermon, her face radiant, her life will suddenly stop, and she will lie there in her coffin, smiling for the scores of friends who come from all over Europe, smiling up at the ceiling, directly into heaven.

Katrina harrison, with her children,
Nicholas and Zofia harrison-Strot

'LET'S GO FOR A DRIVE, REBECCA', I say, and even before we get into the car our game's in full flight. We both know the rules. The first is not to use any English words. That's boring. The second is to talk fast, and the third, to communicate as clearly as we can. It's okay to use our hands. We head out the driveway and up the hill en route to the supermarket and this time I flick on the tape recorder which I keep beside me in case a poem comes when I'm driving:

—Dandra folaheen spindi?
—Nuba, nuba, krob kalla hastie fon shayover.
—Benda krosty foigen denna weeb crasta shobo?
—Phyzalee krempt.
—Din SHTRABA ZEE!??

Incredulous as she asks this last question, she pauses, and looks hard at me, and we both start laughing. We're understanding each other perfectly so far, using our bodies to underline our meanings and the stories we're telling are really funny so we continue like this, taking turns and laughing, all the way into town. On the way back from shopping we record a lot more, and once inside we play the whole thing to Christina and Katrina. They look puzzled and say nothing but we know they think we're both a little mad.

We find it odd that people simply don't understand. To us the whole game seems quite straightforward.

Katrina & Rebecca, 1970

A COLLEAGUE, WHO KNOWS ABOUT these things, advises us at dinner: 'So if you're out in the open and there's no way to escape don't *ever* lie down flat. Some people will say you should, but they're wrong. This thing has no mind and it doesn't know it's you there, so it treats you like a plank and sucks you up, and whirls you round. Then it drops you maybe half a mile away and breaks every bone in your body. So when you see one coming you should roll yourself into a ball and get under something—something like a fence, and hang on. A ball's much harder to suck up into the air than a plank. If you can't find anything to get under, look for a ditch and make yourself as round as possible. That's all you can do.'

A STUDENT HURRIES THROUGH my office door and begins talking even before I ask her to sit down.

— The haiku exercise you assigned is giving me hell. I need some help.

— How so?

— I know it has to be 17 syllables and I've tried every way I can to pare it down but I can't get it lower than 18 and it's driving me cuckoo. I'm stuck. I'm also stuck on where to start.

— Hold on. I don't think I told you a haiku must be 17 syllables. The number 17 doesn't mean anything in poetry in English. It might in Japanese. And, anyway you don't have to write a haiku. Choose any form you want for this exercise.

— But I want to do a haiku, and do it properly.

— All right. What's the chief thing in a haiku?

— Well it has to be about something in nature.

— Maybe. But I think what's most important is a sense of surprise and recognition. What are you writing about?

— Basho and his time in the mountains.

— Fair enough. I haven't read him so I can only make a suggestion. Would that be useful?

— Certainly would.

— Well you might think of Basho as a fictional character and ask yourself some questions about him.

— Such as?

— Well, let's see. Did he suffer from indigestion? Did he dislike his wife? And how did he feel about politicians, or his neighbours? Try anything that gets you going. Does that help?

— Maybe. I'll give it a try.

WHEN I GET TO THE TOP of the rise I drive fast through the STOP sign, accelerate down the hill, turn into the driveway and brake hard. It's midday but the sky's gone black; black with sky-wide bands of green, and rolling thunder as if the air's a field of a thousand armies. I run up the walkway, fling the door open and shout up the stairs: **'WE ALL HAVE TO GET TO THE BASEMENT RIGHT NOW, BRING YOUR BLANKETS, AND SOMETHING TO READ. HURRY!'** and as I do a huge limb snaps off the box-elder beside the house and thumps down the wall. Soon we're squatting on the cellar-stairs as far down into the basement as we can go. The wind-sound gets louder. We're scared. We can hear tree-limbs crashing to the ground all around the house. Last week three houses were pulled off their foundations and the marooned families inside had nowhere to hide. Because our house is in a hollow we might be lucky.

We wrap blankets around us and listen. A water pump whines, then stops, begins again. We tell the children stories, cocoon them as best we can against the mindless beast that's destroying the weatherboard walls around us.

I WAKE WITH A KIND of trickster figure jumping about in my head. Since my student hasn't run with my suggestions I decide to take my own advice. I give a name to my trickster. I call him Basho, after Matsuo Bashō, about whom I know nothing except two poems in a poor translation. In my half-sleep I'd imagined Basho's wife smelling of lotus-blossom, and Basho lost in a dream-stare under a mountain, composing haiku.

That night everyone in my house, including two guests from New York, goes off to a party but I don't want to join them. Instead, I clear the kitchen table, open my notebook and take a drag from a reefer I'd rolled from some grass called Panama Red that my friends brought in from New York, and I begin writing, very fast, some of the lines I'd been hiving in my head since dawn.

My new trickster-figure quickly becomes a friendly companion and he's very smart. My mind's teeming with images and voices and the more I write the more Basho catches me off-guard. When I want to say something serious, the words veer off into nonsense; when I want to be irreverent the poems turn serious and sometimes sad. It's as if I'm chasing something almost out of control. He's too quick for me to keep up with, so I just let him take me where he will. After about three hours I find I've written page after page and have easily enough poems for a small book.

I read them aloud to a friend who loves all things Japanese and he's delighted. I've never written anything with so little effort. Later I add a few new pieces, do some tough editing and am, once again, surprised at the strangeness of these pieces. They're neither imitations nor parodies nor satires; they're in a category of their own. It seems that I'd had nothing to do with them except act as a conduit. It's all very weird, and very gratifying.

I send a complete ms. of *The Basho Poems* to Oxford University Press and, after a few months, receive a very polite letter from my old friend Jon Stallworthy saying how much the editorial board had enjoyed reading the book, adding that they're unfortunately unable to publish the poems because they're 'simply too amusing'. For a mischievous moment I'm tempted to reply that, for generations, Oxford's published a poet called Lord Byron and he, to my best knowledge, wrote amusing poems. I'm also tempted to ask if their letter of rejection was written by Basho.

Instead, I leave the whole thing go.

THE DAY AFTER CHRISTINA and the children leave he's watching me in strong daylight from the back of the sofa and I know, once more, that he's hated me for a long time. I go closer and look into his face and I see an Egyptian god who's all-knowing. His gaze seems to be rammed with the emptiness of the sky.

I go outside and split some wood, feeling the air of the late fall bite my arms. When I'm back inside I remember I've left some keys in the bedroom. I climb the stairs and, while fossicking about in a drawer, glance at my bed and notice something very disturbing. Right in the centre of my pillow, he has shat, brown and yellow, a huge squat, that shouts up at me, *'There, take that!'*

I proceed downstairs, very quietly so as not to make him suspicious, and pour some milk into his bowl and call him *'Tch, tch, tch.'* He approaches the bowl cautiously. I make as if to pour more milk with my left hand but, with my right, clutch the loose fur-flesh at the back of his neck and lift him clear off the floor. I stride outdoors and down to the barn and while he's flailing about at the end of my arm, open the door and, with a forward swing, release him into the dark, and say: 'This is your new home, Lord Byron. Go get some hot rats. We don't need each other any more.'

Lying awake after midnight, I can still hear him breathing out there and I tell him: 'Think me mean if you like, but you've been living in the Siberian steppes for millions of years and you can manage the Minnesota winter very nicely. It will make a man of you.'

I think I have his attention now.

'In any case, it's bastards like you who ruin all the bird-life around here. Every day I find a snarl of robin-feathers or the bones of a cardinal on the grass. You're a rapacious killer, a species of wild-cat intelligent enough to stay small so that soppy people can fondle you and feed you at appointed times for the term of your natural life while all the while you go on thinking: "My god these two-legged creatures are stupid." Then stretch and yawn deliciously in front of the fire we stoke to keep you warm.

'I know you can hear my thoughts as you patrol around the barn.

'What I really respect is your otherness. There's nothing human about you. I admire the way you move like a rhythm of light across the grass, and kill. Your sockets are oiled with a fluid that we humans don't know. When a motor-bike cracks your pelvis, you go to ground, five days without water or food and by some elixir known only to you, you re-join your bones.

'You'll survive the winter and your pelt will grow thick and gleam in the low-angled sun. The barn will be your forest and you'll be entirely wild. Then in spring, when the ground sweats under a thin covering of snow you'll cut yourself and be invaded by a quick infection and the vet will say "Too late, too late."'

And I will take your stiff ruin with its magnificent pelt, pour gasoline over you, and burn you down to nothing in the grass.

5
Crossings

The huge wave bowls me over
churns me in the shingle,
a branch of bladderwrack

hurled shoreward.
Sand in my crotch, I stand up
rejoicing, the Pacific

roaring in my ears,
plunge in again, ram through
the white wall, and make for

darker water. Under my legs
The shark cruises by
and then

the huge wave
trundles me up the shingle;
it was the same wave

took me, years ago,
and I am home —
the same gull hanging

motionless
over me

*

What winds me back
to this wind-blown bay?

        Sixteen years

under fog and snow,
and in that strangeness
found a woman

in a smoky city.
Ten years; affection and confusion;
and found these daughters

who screech
as the edge of the ocean
fizzes over their toes.

What winds me back
where the wind howls
and still

the granite headland butts its nose
like a brown bull in the combers ?

Jess harrison, Katrina, Rebecca & Christina, ca. 1974

VIN BUCKLEY POKES HIS HEAD into my office.

— Listen mate, I meant to ask you at lunch—I've been wondering if you could do me a favour.
— Sure, Vin…

I've come back to Melbourne, but this time on a Fellowship and I feel the old discomfort of being back at this University, where I never really belonged. The strangeness gathers around me and holds me in like an overcoat. I have a book to finish and my aging parents need me here right now. I also have two daughters in Minneapolis depending on me. Vin doesn't know anything about all that.

— Sure, Vin—what can I do?
— Well, each year I do something that they call the 'Yeats Lecture' and I have a lot of visitors as well as my own students. It's open to the public—but I can't do it this year. Have to be in Sydney for five days. I'm wondering if you could possibly stand in for me. I know you like Yeats.

I'm deeply flattered, and very surprised. During my absence in England and America, Vin's achieved a sturdy reputation here, as a poet, and a much-loved teacher. What he's proposing is a tall order.

— When's the lecture?
— Next Tuesday.
— That's only four days.
— I know. I'm really sorry to drop this on you at short notice.

I think a moment.
— Vin, I'm really honored that you've asked me but I have a problem. I'm going through some personal stuff in Minnesota at the moment. My head's not in a good place, but I'll think

hard about it—and I'll give you an answer this evening.
— Fair enough.

Vin turns down the corridor and I start figuring. It so happens that I've been making notes for a special lecture on Yeats, concentrating on two of his late collections. Maybe I can bring it all together in time, but I'll have to hurry. I make some quick notes and things begin to fall into place. Just before five I knock on Vin's door and when he opens it I say 'Okay Vin, I'll do it.'
— Great! What will you lecture on?
— I think I'll concentrate on *The Winding Stair* and *The Tower*—how they complement each other.
— Very interesting. I was going to look at a few poems in *The Tower*, so that'll do perfectly. Good on you, and thanks a lot.

I go back to my study and work hard for several days.

*

Come Tuesday I find myself standing at the lectern in front of about four hundred people who have no idea who I am, and I say 'Vin Buckley's asked me to stand in for him and no one can do that, but I'm going to try.'

Many luminaries have stood in this spot and I should be nervous but I have Willie Yeats' poems to help me and I begin by booming out one of my favorites without looking at the text and I have their immediate attention because my voice carries better than I expected in this immense room. Yeats, whose whole life was spent trying to write memorable verse, can do this to an audience. Right now I'm merely his emanation.

I look up from my notes, and survey the huge crowd in the auditorium.
— Can you all hear me—especially those of you up there in the back?

No one says *No*, and most nod.

— Good, I want you to hear everything because all the words in these late poems are essential.

I share another short poem which I assume they probably don't know:

> *You think it horrible that lust and rage*
> *Should dance attention upon my old age.*
> *They were not such a plague when I was young.*
> *What else have I to spur me into song?*

I pause a moment and give them the poem again.

— This poem isn't in either of the collections I'm discussing today, but it's a clue to something important in Yeats. One of the things that prompted him was what he called 'original sin'. In the poem I just read he calls it 'lust and rage.' Particularly as he got older, Yeats believed that all the ideas in the world can be blown completely away when he stands before a beautiful young woman, and his only thought is:

> *O that I was young again and held her in my arms.*

I go on to explain, with all kinds of examples and a few whole poems, that what grabbed and held Yeats was the very stuff of life itself. He was concerned, particularly as he got older with being alive, in all its imperfections, right here, right now.

I pause. They're listening.

— But that's only half the story. The other half can be gathered under a general complex of ideas which Yeats called Byzantium.

I go on to explain some of the things that Yeats implies by that name. This takes quite a few minutes and some diagrams on the huge blackboard. Then I make a stop.

— Any questions so far?

There's a slight pause then someone near the back pipes up: 'No, you're doing well. Keep going', and everyone laughs but the laughter's friendly.

'Okay', I say, 'but I want to make an aside and I think Vin Buckley would agree with me. For Yeats there's an important dimension in poetry that I haven't mentioned. You all know the French word *oui*. Does anyone know what it comes from?'

Immediately a young woman calls out: 'From the old verb *ouir*.'
—And what's it mean?

Someone else calls out: 'It means "to hear".'
— Good. So what does that imply?
— It means when you say *'oui'* you're really saying *'heard'* —or *'I understand'*.

For a moment I have the sense that, if I keep asking the right questions, the students can learn just as much from each other as they can from me, but I go on to say: 'For Yeats, hearing a poem is essential. Right now we don't *hear* poems, we *read* them. And our eyes, on their own, miss a great deal. Yeats fought against that kind of deafness all his life. He wanted us to understand his poems by their being carried along on their music. What we really should be doing today is booming out all the key poems in *The Winding Stair* and *The Tower*, not just *talking* about them. There are too many of us for that, and I have a plane to catch — so you'll just have to allow me to perform them for you. I want to leave you with something useful as quickly as I

147

can. But I do recommend you read the poems aloud in your own time. And please read them slowly. Our eyes are always too impatient and we cheat ourselves, and the poet. You may not believe me but I'm sure this is true: when you read poems aloud you begin to understand them for the first time.'

I look up again and am gratified. I've gained their full attention. There's something magical about this room. It has very friendly presences, so I continue building my essential argument and reading the poems as well as I can. I try to show that Yeats is torn between a desire to be a golden bird singing in Byzantium, but he's *also* pulled back, time and again, to the joys and the imperfections of living here, fully in the body. The tension between these two things, I explain, is almost intolerable and that's the real key to the poems in these two volumes, and to nearly all his later poetry. 'If Yeats had left us only the early dreamy stuff such as *The Lake Isle of Innisfree* that most people associate him with, we wouldn't pay him much attention', I say.

I go on reading the poems letting them speak for themselves, making a few comments, and fielding questions, then I glance at the clock and realize I have to round the lecture off, so I do that by saying: 'One of the chief ways we can measure the greatness of Yeats is to say that it's in the tension with which he holds together these two absolutely contradictory elements of his thought that the full strength of the late poetry reveals itself. It's as if he's stretching the string of a violin almost to breaking-point, but it still holds. It's in that tension his imagination catches fire.'

I've so enjoyed introducing this large audience of young people to Yeats that, for a moment, I lose track of where I am. I've been swimming in the sound of these late poems and I've apparently taken at least some of my listeners with me on that journey.

When I lift my gaze the students for a brief moment are quite still. It's as if they're not looking at me, but beyond me. Then quite suddenly, as a body, to my very considerable surprise, they begin to stand, and applaud. That's never happened to me before and I'm quite overwhelmed. I make my way to the door, give a wide-swinging wave and hurry to the car park where my father and brother are waiting to drive me to the airport, from where I'll head for Sydney and then, next day, back to my old farm-house near Minneapolis.

Outside, not far from the Old Arts Building, my brother's car is idling at the kerb-side.

I get in.

'Well, how did it go, son?' My father asks.

'Not bad, I say. Not bad.'

A MEMBER OF THE SENIOR FACULTY bursts out of his office into the corridor and shouts to no one in particular, *'What are they all protesting for—this doesn't concern them!'* He turns his gaze on me, and I have an answer: 'I think it does concern them. For one thing they don't want to die in some jungle thousands of miles from here—especially for something they don't believe in.'

— Nonsense, they should be in class, not out here. They're just making fools of themselves. They're all too wet behind the ears to understand.

— Well, I think they're acting very responsibly, and I'm joining them.

With a loud *harrumph!* He turns back into his office and I hurry to the centre of the quadrangle behind the chapel where a large, untidy, badly-dressed and boisterous crowd of young men and women are standing around, some on boxes making speeches. They're passionate and intelligent. They simply don't believe in the reasons they've been given for this war.

Later, in a downtown bar, I'm joined by my new friends Bob Tisdale, Bob Bonner and Tommy Rosin and we find we share the students' views. The war has no clear purpose and even a cursory glance at a topographical map shows how difficult it would be to 'win' a war in Vietnam—whatever that might mean. After all, the French, with a cracker army, were sent packing ignominiously years ago.

The four of us, helped by a number of beers, make plans to encourage the students in their cause.

Next day the students call a campus-wide meeting in Great Hall. Three of them make formal and beautifully crafted speeches against the War, which conclude with their setting fire to their draft cards. The tension is electric. This is the real thing and it's very dangerous. Students from all over the country, out of fear of the draft, have already migrated to Canada. The fate of those who remain is unknown. But the three students in this body—David Loy, Paul Smith and Harold Henderson—before they burn their cards, lay out their reasons for going against their country in a way which is unforgettable.

Tommy and both Bobs and I spend the next months helping our students speak, write, and act against the war wherever we can. By this time we've become fast friends and we see ourselves as the young Turks on the faculty and are regarded with disdainful indifference by many of our colleagues. We organize marches to the nearby military base; Bob Bonner goes off with a student delegation to make his anti-war case in Paris; Bob Tisdale teaches special courses on the literature of war, and all of us talk to anyone who will listen, about the futility and the horror of the conflict in Vietnam.

With the War finally over except for its horrifying aftermath, the four of us resume our normal lives of teaching, research and writing. Tommy, as an anthropologist in Rajasthan, begins a lifelong project of writing a new kind of anthropology which is in sharp contrast to the prevailing mode of detached documentation. His research is based on stories and vivid encounters with the Rajasthani villagers whose lives he begins to understand intimately and whose language he speaks fluently. Bob Bonner, after many years as a scholar and teacher of Elizabethan History, in his later years turns his mind to the history of his own state, Wyoming and, among other things, produces a book on Buffalo Bill, for which he's acknowledged by his own alma mater with an honorary degree. Over many years he's become master of a prose-style which few of his fellow-historians can rival. Bob Tisdale, throughout a long and distinguished career, makes his mark as teacher of such skill that thousands of students remember his classes with affection and gratitude. His teaching style, built on the subtlest and wisest pedagogical principles, is *sui generis*. No one has been able to discover the secrets on which it's built.

These three colleagues have been my solid friends for many years. Three of us are now in our ninth decade and one in his tenth. We've raised our families, spent our seasons in hell, experienced the death of loved ones and are still standing, *compos mentis*, perhaps a little more quietly than we used to, and we often rejoice in that.

*

Many years after the three young men burnt their draft cards in Great Hall, in my last year on the faculty, I'm asked to greet the incoming freshmen with a poem and I choose that earlier incident and the mindless terror and slaughter in Vietnam as my focus. I write a poem addressed to my then students about my own 'freshman' year as a member of the faculty:

> In my freshman year the fury of Vietnam
> broke out, and we woke up in hell. I remember
> a gathering in Great Hall, late September,
> where three young men rose up, each with a story
> that deeply questioned the old, unquestioned tag:
> *Dulce et decorum est pro patria mori.*
> Their voices steady, they accepted their task,
> their sentences complete, knowing the risk,
> they spoke out, then struck a match and burned the cards
> which ordered them to march beneath a flag
> and offer up their lives for another's words
> and the flames in their hands replied: *Non serviam.*
>
> Standing beside the president of the College
> I studied his face: he was concerned, then suddenly proud
> that three young men, be they right or wrong,
> with such clean manliness, though they be flayed
> by parents, teachers, and an ignorant throng,
> should so resist. I was young. Those men were in my
>   charge.
> My head was crammed with another kind of knowledge;
> they would soon be vilified for theirs, but they were large
> in spirit, and they would not be cowed

by those who reproached them with unthinking zeal,
for they had found their center, and it tasted real.
I thought them unimpeachable. That is why I stayed.

Not one student in this freshman audience was alive at the time of the Vietnam War so my purpose in this Convocation is to remind them of what happened back then, here at this College. Like it or not, that's their heritage. I have no idea what effect it has on them. Maybe they take it as a piece of fustian cultural archeology as remote as the Punic Wars.

What we do know is that these recent years have given us something much more terrifying than Vietnam: a criminally irresponsible and ignorant President of the U.S. who's taken us much further into chaos and incoherence than Richard Nixon ever dreamed possible.

HE KNOWS WITHOUT MY TELLING HIM. Betrayed. He strides to-ward me and gives a huge bear-hug. 'I know', he says. 'You're alone, and it stinks', and I'm trying like hell not to cry.

This time by Bess, companion of three years, who has turned sharply away. Bess who, in betrayal, has the amazing virtue of luminous innocence. After four marriages she smiles and smiles. Her face shines with joy. Everything is just FINE. Such innocence is a totally American thing, and utterly disarming. I cannot think of anything more galling than to be betrayed by someone whose face is, and will stay, radiant with joy.

Outside, the fall night is deep and windless.

Jim and I are Celts in exile. We carry about us a sense of humus and the untidy hubbub of the tribe, its music and its stories. A tribe that, apart from phone-calls to Australia and Ireland, is largely absent here, on this windy plain between two huge rivers. In America there is no sense of the tribe. There are peo-ple in large boxes but you cannot see them; and people, mostly hidden, in cars. No one walks the roads on foot or works in the fields. People connect with electronic antennae. Some of the larger houses alongside the golf-course have inter-comms in every room. The family members are always looking for each other. Everything smells clean and people are terribly alone.

In this isolation Jim is your brother. He and his gracious south-ern wife, Jane, have become fast friends and they welcome me almost as a family-member into their house. Jim takes me to see a head-doctor because I'm fearful of the fires of self-destruc-tion. In spite of urgencies at home he stays with me all day. He knows all about this. He has been in the same place and come out of it almost whole. He stays with me in the hospital all day, not speaking because there is little to say.

This is hell nor am I out of it.

154

Silent words fill the silence.

As a young man Jim took a journey in his head, away to Cambridge, but his body accompanied him reluctantly. There, among old English stones, the tribal voice grew an overlay of southern English civility, but neither in England or America has he ever really moved from his roots in the black earth of Ireland. He teaches literary theory and Shakespeare and for a while was seduced by the priests of the Ecole Normale and a distinctly French form of obfuscation. But he soon recovered from all that. Now, once again—nearing retirement—there is something about him that's primitive and essential. He gives and receives affection with great ease and humour. He smells of peat.

AT PIRRA THE KANGAROOS sometimes come up to the kitchen fence at dusk and resume their boxing.

Geoffrey's new place is a huge Victorian mansion dating back to the early 19th century with an open garden and a few sheep whom Geoffrey regards as 'really intelligent', an idea that's never crossed my mind.

He's built a theatre in an old machine-shed and now, instead of teaching in the city he has dozens of school-kids visit for day-long classes to perform the small operas he writes for them. Geoffrey's a dynamo who combines gardening, carpentry, re-building old cars and composing and making music.

One evening while we're watching the kangaroos, Geoffrey turns to me and says:

— Let's do a performance suite.

— Sounds fine. What do you have in mind?

— Well, I want to include poetry, music, actors and dancers.

— Go on.

— Look, we have marvellous birds, right here, next door in the Sanctuary: blue-faced herons, magpies, brolgas—kookaburras, and a lot more. I think we should celebrate them in a piece for the stage. So let's go study them. What do you say? I want something varied, like a carnival. A kind of technicolour romp. Can you write us some words?

— How many pieces?

— Oh, about five or six.

— Okay. I'll give it a try.

On the flight back to Minnesota, high above the Pacific, I begin the lyrics for *The Birds at Pirra* and by the time I arrive I have a rough draft. I send it to Geoffrey and we work at it hard for several weeks. Back at Pirra, we try them on the stage, then with live audiences, then in Minneapolis and, much later, Geoffrey and the Pirra Ensemble take them to Chile and other places in South America.

Some of the pieces are droll, some quiet and reflective and some, like the one we call *Kookaburra Kanon* is pure fun:

Geoffrey O'Ombrain. ca. 1990

Kookaburra Kanon

Begin voice 1   Begin voice 2

Voices

Hey, Jack!   Mock - a cass o - war - y, jack - a - napes crack a ber - ry (ka

ka)   cook a black snake in your bomb bel - ly, mer - ry cock - y mot - tled rub - ber rob - ber slap - stick

(ka___ ka ka   ) brown and   round___ as a prow - ling owl   (ka   ka ka

) cook - ie   crack - er mac - ca knock - er oc - cer back - er snap   smack   snake a -

gainst the flat rock brake his back like a foot - y sock and yank him up   (ka   ka ka)   flap

to the tree - tops, slump - ing all sum - mer with your tum - my on your bum   (ka ka

) health - y as an ap - ri - cot wealth - y as a Rom - an slut stealth - y as a youn go-

an - na   track   the mis - ty morn - ing in your yel - low   eye   Hey jack   mock a

cass - o - war - y   (ka - ko)   KIK - KU - kuk - a - bum

ko - ki   kay - ko   (ka   )   Hey, jack!

CHRISTINA.

Is.

Not my wife. Is.

Because our children. Etched in the bones: no flint-stone can erase the signatures. *Wife, wave, weave.* Made our children. Bred them. *Brood, broth, bread.* Good words. Belonging. Is their mother. Was our daughters' mother. Is.

Stands there yanking the leash of her huge huskie. And our daughters climbing into their womanhood. New York, Melbourne, Minneapolis. Phone-calls, ice-wind, new children, hair flaming as their mother's, and their mother's father's father's. Ireland, Cornwall. Out of tin-mines, out of the apple-slopes of Tasmania, out of the white hell-wastes near Jøtenheimen, on and on.

What wind out of a Viking hell blew her to Malcolm's house, and mine? To ours, to mine?

Years contracting as the coffee brews. The Christmas tree is real again. The red-wax candles still dangerous in this huge wooden house. Thirty years. It is the same wind heaves through Minnesota and all of time, and Nikos, the huskie, yowling to go out and bite it.

Courage from her straight-backed mother, a certain stoic pride. Ice in the belly, when the days go black with anger and disappointment. Knows heat. The vivid heat of being herself.

Wife, womb, woman. Today, the winds of *Was* and *Is* all blow from the self-same place.

DEEP IN THE SNOWY MOUNTAINS thousands of miles from Min-
nnesota, I'm getting ready to slide into my sleeping bag, when I
think of my grandkids, Nicholas and Zofia, and a poem comes.
I go to sleep having shaped it in my mind. In the morning I set
it down:

(KIDS)
surge like white water round
our legs and round the kitchen;
they ram wedges of apple-pie
between their teeth, leaving
bits all over the plate, then bugger off
to shinny up the plum-tree, giggling
so hard they terrify the magpies.
they dunk bread-bits in their Milo,
sprint through the sprinkler, shouting
Hell with you and hell with you.

Inside again, they scrinch their noses up
and belch, twice, just as Beethoven
rises to Nirvana. Kids run everywhere
wearing grape-leaves in their hair, snot
dangling from their noses.
                    Green sap
simmering in their bones, kids
renew us each day with their shrieks
and questions, the way their limp
limbs hang over the bed-cliffs, dopey
with dawnlight as we lift them
up to our hearts, smelling of salt
tidewater flats, and bread-loaves
hot from the oven.

Nicholas & Zofia, ca. 2001

HE RANGES THROUGH THE LARGE HOUSE with its high-headed rooms and stained glass. Misplaced his music again. Rummages in cupboards and desks, muttering to himself as if he believes that the lost piece will leap out of the detritus of fifty years of composing, teaching, arranging, recording, acting, stage-managing and whatnot—will leap out and say 'Here I am, Geoffrey, exactly where you thought!'

The music in question is the first movement of Bach's flute sonata in B Minor, BWV 1030 from the amazing suite for flute and harpsichord.

— I've got half of it, but the part I can't find's a bit complicated, and it's a while since I played it. I just have to find it for tonight.

He goes on fossicking in drawers, and cupboards.

The opening movement, which is what he's looking for, is quite quick, yet it has a suave assuredness, along with very deft dynamics in the rhythm. Just as you're getting used to a steady pattern, Bach introduces dynamics of rhythm that make the inner ear twitch with curiosity. The piece is intensely alive and it presents a tough challenge for a flautist. It requires a mastery of breathing and phrasing.

— Why tonight?
— I've got to play it for some ladies down at the coast. I promised them last year. They're all very keen, and they know Bach to the bone.
— How will you play it if you can't find the music?
— I don't know. I'll have to do it somehow.

He continues shifting papers from desk to desk, and muttering.

WHEN SHE HEARS MY STEP along the garden walkway she looks up from under her mauve hat with its enormous rim, and grins. 'I know you,' she says, 'I met you last year, and you wrote the Basho Poems—I had such a good time reading them'. I'm immediately taken with the mischievous flash of her brown eyes. 'They call me Dottie', she says. 'But I'm not—not completely, anyway.' She grins broadly, wipes her hand on her pinafore, shakes mine, then shows me around her sod-house, where they cornered a skunk two years ago and it sprayed everything, especially the dog. The earthen walls still carry the smell. She laughs.

— I tell you, we bathed the dog in gallons of tomato-juice every day for a week, and he still stank. Makes you believe in God. Only something with superhuman intelligence could design such over-kill.

Again, she laughs from her belly, a laugh which seems to come from under the earth. Her voice is contralto and very musical.

In the twilight she tells me about her mother and the things she loved and how the family buried her. She tells me about choke-cherries, and the spring which bubbles up into a pool so clear that it grows water-cress, which will only tolerate the purest water.

After the hell of divorce, followed by months of solitude, in the green fields and soft hills of Wisconsin where the sugar-bush grows tall, these people who have chosen to live close to the land surround me with the gifts of acceptance and healing. The iced-over locks in my spirit begin to break apart. I smell the cow-dung and the rain, and all around me there's a new flowing. Dottie knows all that and she takes me into her house and family.

163

Summer comes and I write a poem for her and her mother,
about whom she's told me many stories:

You buried your mother
under the belly of the hill.
You did not ask permission:
carried her there, hacked out a hole
and planted her,
then planted a plum-tree over her.
Each year you light a ring of candles
and sing the songs she cared for.
You sing in joy, standing on
her body, and the song goes down from your toes
and into her bones, the city
of insects and minerals and living things
she is quietly becoming.

*

I woke this morning thinking of her
whom I never saw.
Last night, a hungry deer
dragged at her tree
with his blind teeth, and killed it.
You laughed when you saw the tooth-cuts:
She would have enjoyed his hunger —
The animal, obeying himself.

You will plant another tree in her:
crab-apple, cherry — they'll bloom,
or the deer will savage them.
Let it be.

*

Our daughters bloom
in the late
sunlight and water splashed
on their quick bodies.

Stripped off our stale clothes
plunged with them
down to the floor of the dark pool
among the mud-slime and the pecking fish
rose up blowing spray
rinsing the shadows from our brains
roved like dolphins through
the blue space of summer
enjoying hunger
work of our hands and backs
belly of the cow pulsing
against our cheeks,
the house climbing the hill like coral
the white moon striding over us
as we slept with the crickets in the juicy grass.

*

Woke this morning, thinking
beauty is, yes, of body.
A thousand books fell from my mind,
Leaving only the pattern on the pinewood ceiling.
Thought of the deer's teeth,
our daughters, their small
breasts budding, their shyness —
and then we walked on the living grass
over your mother's body

over the bones of many people:
mothers and sisters and exhausted soldiers —
over all our brothers sleeping under the hill.

*

Tonight at Bubbling Springs the table's heaped for Thanksgiving. We're not eating turkey, but red meat from the farm. There must be fifteen different dishes on the table. Carrots like little flames in white bowls, slabs of corn-bread, still steaming from the oven, basins of lettuce dotted with radishes, red and white corn, five minutes from the cob. Dottie turns to me, a twinkle in her eye:

—How did you like that steak?

—Rich, but a little chewy.

—That's Ernie, she says, and laughs. Ernie was a really tough son of a gun.

YOU HAVE TO STUDY IT for years before you see them. You have to sweep your eyes along the horizon, then almost down to your toes, from the scraggle of farm-sheds to the left of the easel, there by County 21, with its silo of hard navy-blue, right down to the lost creek with a clump of aspens by Olafson's house. I'm talking about the whales. You never quite see them but they're almost there, heaving just below the surface. You sense them more under the soles of your feet than with your eyes. Month after month you try with stubs of charcoal to get inside this landscape with its whales. You try not so much to draw the countryside but *write* it, across long sheets of paper. Everything comes out flat and dumb.

There's nothing breathing in these sketches.

Then one day right after lunch I turn my van's nose away from the College and pull into a clump of trees and begin working the charcoal in a different way: broad sweeps almost a metre long in a kind of dance that pulls my hand with it, and after a few minutes I turn, and when I stand back I see I've made a leap and, in a tiny way, for the first time I'm *inside* the land. Just a bit, but it's a start. In a few minutes the sketch finishes itself and I lean it against a fence-post, and stand back.

It's awful. Yet it's pulsing with clumsy, promising life. I've broken through. All the bad years fall into place and a fizz of excitement runs through my body and, once again, Hopkins' words come racing back:

> *Each mortal thing says one thing and the same:*
> *Selves, goes of itself. For that I came.*

Now there's only one thing to do. Quickly I put the sketch book in my haversack and turn the car back toward college, into my parking-slot beside the library. I stride up the stairs to the president's office where Miss Whittaker immediately finds a time for me.

'YOU LOOK VERY CHEERFUL', President Galbraith says as he opens the door.

— I am, sir. I am. But I can't quite tell you why.

— Well, give it a shot.

— This afternoon I found out why I came.

— And why was that?

— I discovered the whales.

— Whales? Out here in Minnesota?

— Yes. It's difficult to explain.

— Come on now. You're never short of words. Tell me more.

— Okay. All these years standing in front of my classes, taking notes at meetings, reading papers and exams, buckling myself into a suit and tie, I've felt like an impostor.

— How so?

— Don't get me wrong, I've loved the work, and I love this college and my students and this town — you've all been much kinder to me than I deserve — but, hell how can I say this? It's not really what I want to be doing. I want to do a lot more writing and sketching. I'm at last getting to know the landscape. It's alive in a way I never quite saw before, though I've been close. So I have to make a change as soon as I can. There are four more days till the end of term, and then I'm off. You're the first one I've told.

— Well, this is a surprise.

— Certainly is. I'm still not sure I'm standing here saying all this.

I turn through the door, past Miss Whittaker, who smiles.

And if I didn't run back to my car, drive home and complete that sketch and keep on trying to capture this country I'd been studying so long, I must have climbed the stairs directly from my car, by-passed the president's office, gone into my book-heavy eyrie on the third floor and plunged my head into a pile of essays and lost myself while four more years slowly ran down, and ran me down, and I never looked once at my sketches until just now, and after all the mortgages and the broken house and the confusion of the years, I can see the big whales once again, still there, still heaving under the tide-swells of the corn and I take a chunk of charcoal and begin moving with the whales and I say to myself *They're still breathing, and there's time. You can make friends with them again. But this time you have to keep your hand moving, you have to begin again writing them with wide sweeps, and sometimes a silent whiteness that's alive. Black, and white, and everything between. You have to make your stub of charcoal go on singing.*

THE QUESTION COMES BACK AGAIN: *what's the shortest stanza you can devise in English — one that can also be used for a long poem?*

The question won't be shaken away.

I flick on the desk-light and begin doodling in my note-pad. I continue for many minutes but the doodles come to nothing. Then I think of Dante, who liked the number three, and I also think about syllables. Auden made some great poems using syllabics. *So let's forget about feet and stresses and all that, and try something new. What about a stanza of 3-5-3?*

More doodles, and this time, as I consider the seasons here in southern Victoria something happens. There are more than four seasons in Australia. For a start, there's early autumn, and late autumn. They're entirely different. Yesterday, here at Pirra, something happened as I made my way to the theatre for a rehearsal. I pick up my pen and write

> *Faster than*
> *shot-pellet or a*
> *sprung sling-shot,*
>
> *a sharp bird*
> *stabs an apricot.*
> *the rot starts.*

The poem comes so quickly that I don't notice at first that the syllables are talking to each other: there are four '*ot*' sounds in 22 syllables, and other sounds that seem to echo each other. *I'm onto something here*, I think and turn my mind to other seasons in Australia, then to a beautiful woman in Minnesota waking early in first spring:

> *Morning flares*
> *in the curtains. Quick,*
> *wake up, take*

me now. I
will be ravished in
lilac-light.

Then a late fall image floats into mind: the valley near where
the St. Croix River meets the Mississippi and the whole forest,
for a few days, is completely transformed:

Green burns down
in urns of burnished
umber gold —

as if a
sultan's roof turned to
copper flames.

Soon my notebook's brimming with poems celebrating the seasons on the two continents I've been living in all these years.
Some drafts go into the WPB, but some seem to be keepers. I
discover that, for reasons I can't explain, syllabics, like sonnets,
couplets and quatrains, can help concentrate the music of our
thoughts. What holds me right now is this new 11-syllable stanza, especially when it's doubled:

Jealousy
has so fine an ear
it can catch

the creak of
bedsprings, clear across
five counties.

After a dozen or so of these miniatures I'm having such a fine
time I want to thank someone— but who? It must be the ghost
of Pythagoras, who also liked numbers and geometry, and I
find myself writing in a more playful mode:

This little
wavering dance of
threes and five

fits me well.
It keeps my flatfoot
wits alive…

Then I stop.

Verse again, I say to myself. *You don't want to bother with* feet, *for god's sake! The end-stopped rhyme on 'five' and 'alive' makes the poem lock back into itself. Wrong move! You want to make the whole thing drive **forward**—you want to keep everything open.* I cross out the last word, think a moment, and try another two-syllable word:

…It keeps my flatfoot
*wits **jumping**…*

That little change makes all the difference. Now the rhythm's got real energy and the words continue flowing down the page

…It can flick
fast as a tomtit's
tail — or move

extremely
slow, like mauve seaweed
pulsing in

a green sea.
Here, one small word can
swell, to a

landscape wide
as Minnesota,
or even

wider — say
to the blind dark of
Milton's Hell.

A certain
mathematical
imp or spell

hides in it;
most anything goes
within its

free confines:
Pop, Be-bop, jumped up
Reggae bump

bums against
Karlheinz Stockhausen
and Berio.

If Dante
had found this thinned down
version

instead of
terza rima he'd
have wet his

pants. Just think
of the eyes saved and the
printer's ink!

This new form has me listening to every sound and I realize, again, how much I've learnt from Pound. His political views were unquestionably repulsive, but his ear for verbal nuance and rhythm was as sharp as a fox's. He's helping me, along with a weird kind of game with numbers, to find a new kind of liberation. It's as if I've invented a tight cage for myself and it's very useful because I keep breaking out of it. And, all the time, it still holds. I don't really understand it.

*

The demands of making syllabics prompt me to keep a tape-recorder beside me in the van so I can work on all my drafts, then play them back when I get home, or erase them with a flick of the switch. So I look forward to driving, and especially to long drives. I can work without distractions. I can 'see' and hear the shape of the small stanzas very easily as I drive, and still watch the road. So I make up scores of poems, throw many away, and very shortly I have a gathering of work I want to keep.

Then, just as suddenly as it began, the impulse to write syllabics stops. Except for one piece, which stays in hiding for many months.

MY MOTHER FOUGHT AGAINST HER DEATH to the very end. She was only a slip of a woman but her grit was remarkable. When she finally succumbed, a poem came quickly and I called it ACE.

We were there, all three of us.
For days now she'd been floating.
Not one word.
You could hear though, by the breathing,
she was fighting. This one was tough.
But she was still in charge.

She never believed in loss
of clarity. *That's nonsense.*

Each evening when her sister came
and forgot the one spot where
she stowed her sherry, she scolded her:
But Peg, I showed you yesterday,
and the day before, and the day before.
She refused to think that people
who lose their memory
cannot remember things.

That stubbornness walked with her
almost a hundred years.
On the court when you thundered down an
                              ace
she'd nod, and cross to the other side.
She ran down almost everything you fired at
                              her
and placed it again, and again, until you
                              cracked.

That night — you could hear it in her
                                        breathing —
She was beginning to admit
for the first time, *All right, All right,*
looks like you might outlast me.

As the dialogue with whomever
began to change its tone
we made a circle, six arms
around our mother, and we listened.
The quarrel intensified, then a sudden
sharp intake, a grunt of surprise.

Clear ace.
And she crossed to the other side.

THE DAY AFTER CHRISTINA and the children leave, he leaps onto me and, even through the bed-sheet, sets his teeth so hard into the flesh around my knee-cap that, astonished and deeply scared, all I can do is try to pull him away, but his nails are hooked into my forehead just above my right eye. I hurl myself out of the bed. He's grafted to me so tight that disengaging him is like trying to tear a ball of burdock spikes out of a sweater. I stand in the room while he thrashes against me and I know if I pull him off too suddenly I'll lose my eye. In a black fury I think of a thing to do. With my right hand I grab him by the crotch, squeeze hard, and lift him. For a tiny moment he weakens his grip and I snatch him off me and hurl him at the wall. I hear him thump against it, slump, then slink off into a darkness which is all his own.

I run to the bathroom, sweating heavily. Terrified, I flick on the light to examine the wound in my forehead which smarts as if someone's scraping sandpaper against the bone. There's nothing there. In the mirror my face is white but the flesh is whole. Unbelieving, I reach down to my knee, expecting to find bloody gouges but, again, there's nothing unusual. I begin to cry, then I walk about the house looking for a cigarette, find one, light it and squat by the dumb TV trying to think.

The blackness tells me nothing. Confused, still rubbing my leg, I go back to the bedroom and stand listening. I can't see him, but I know he's still there, lord of the dark, watching my every move. He will choose exactly when to emerge, when to kill.

I can't see him, but I hear him breathing, everywhere.

—YOU LOOK REALLY AWFUL. Bad night?

— You hear anything about three?

— No. Why? What happened?

— I hurled the cat against the wall, and I thought you might have heard it.

— What? We don't have a cat.

— Lord Byron.

— What's Lord Byron got to do with it?

— That's the cat. I killed him. It was a helluva night, Geoffrey. The most intense —

— I know. I had this fantastic dream about a horse a couple of nights ago, a really huge horse, *but that wasn't this cat* froth coming out of his nostrils and he was choking, couldn't breathe, so I had to re-arrange the whole bedroom, very quickly, and lever his head on top of a book-case *but that wasn't this cat*, so he could get some air, and after a while he was okay and I rode him out the door. Do you want some toast?

— No, I'm trying to understand something, and it's difficult. We have a problem. We're old friends and we're not really talking.

— Well, look who's here! *and I also want to talk about this cat, Geoffrey, the one that*—Come on in, Darrin! We're just finishing breakfast. Pull up a chair. I was explaining about this huge horse that couldn't breathe and I had to prop his head on a bookshelf in my bedroom.

'UNLESS WE HAVE A LOT OF LUCK', I say to my grandson, Nicholas, 'the whole thing will be out of whack.' The tree-house we're trying to build has a major problem: the branch-angles are so complex that we can't seem to get anything close to square. Another difficulty: the tree's still growing so we want to make our house 'float' and, at the same time, hold secure. We pause to discuss what to do and I notice the look of concentration on Nick's face, and the blueness of his eyes. A new poem suddenly springs out, and that evening I grab a pad and pencil and set it down:

My father
taught me the ways of
knots and tools;

he showed me
how to whip a rope
with an old

marling-spike
he'd salvaged from his
years at sea.

he'd tuck the
loose whippings under,
pull them firm

and the frayed
ends would tighten, stiff
as a stick.

Almost with
awe he'd touch the tongues
of chisels

and jackplanes.
He loved the feel and
tang of wood.

His plane hissed
down the long oak-grain
spinning thin

shavings up
through the sun-shafts in
his workshop.

Then he'd squint
down the plank, muttering
to himself.

He taught me
all the knots he knew,
and they are

beautiful:
sheep-shank, Garrick bend,
Clove hitch — all

their forms like
fluent signatures
each with its

character
and purpose. I
practise them

now, with my
grandson, Nicholas.
He's four. We're

Working-men
taking a breather.
I wonder

if he'll learn
these old disciplines
although, as

for the knots,
I rarely use them — yet,
when we were

lost last month
in a black sea-storm
my clove-hitch

held the mad
sweep-oar we rigged to
turn us home.

The tools, though,
are another thing.
I keep them

oiled and honed:
imperatives from
my father.

Ninety-four,
his handgrip still like
tempered steel,

I call him
for his birthday: ten
thousand miles.

Good-day, there,
He says. Still got it ?
'What ?'
                    That knife

I lent you
Last year. Still use it ?
'Yep'.
Good. Keep

it sharp, now.
'Don't worry. Hone it
Every day.'

He tells me
he plans to build a
boat with wings

to lift planes
downed at sea. He thinks
of the dead.

'Terrific,'
I say, 'Send me all
your sketches.'

I hang up.
We're lying about
the knife. That

was '60,
maybe '61.
I lost it

moving house,
somewhere in England.
We both know

I'll never
find it now.
                    A man
who touched words

sparingly,
he told me: 'Tools are
the point where

geometry
meets nature: always
difficult.

Respect it.'
That was his own, and
almost worth

the years of
solitude, the pain
he never

shook away.
With respect, I hand
my grandson

his birthday
hammer and we bang
nails into

our new house
that's rising in the
cedar-fork

with the birds
and spiders. I watch
his face as,

frowning, he
concentrates, and I
remember

the clear blue
gaze of my father —
at four, and

ninety four.

I call this one *Builders* and, having written nothing much for quite a while, I'm pleased that it says what I was after.

—Did you find the music?

— No. Ransacked the whole house. It's disappeared.

— So how did you play the Bach?

— Well, since there was nothing I could do about it, I just started playing, and when I got to the end of the part that I could remember, something clicked and I found I had the whole thing in my head. It went marvelously. The women loved it.

I'm so amazed I don't say anything.

— You still look a bit disgruntled. What's up?

— All that bad stuff I was trying to tell you about yesterday. I do think we have a bit of a problem, you and

Geoffrey gets up to fetch the toast

— anyway, one of the woman down there at the coast was a very good muso and she was absolutely gorgeous and

please listen I want to talk to you

— she asked me back to her place by the sea after the performance and we were immediately — yeah, okay, stop smiling, no, I tell you we were immediately simpatico *when I tried to pull him off me about three in the morning I thought I was over the edge and you're not listening that's the problem especially when I hurled him against the wall and why should you because I'm not speaking only listening* and she had a brother who was a student of mine and I tell you she was something else and she's coming here on Thursday, and you'll love her. I'm going to make a Tuscan salad excuse me I think that's the phone *and I went back to bed without a single scratch and lay there hard awake and kept asking myself what is it with this cat and now you've put the phone down*

— What is it with this cat, Geoffrey?

— Cats? They know a lot more than we think. They visit only

184

when they want to. A bit like birds. Nick and I were out in the paddock the other day and for some reason I put my hand up and, no kidding, a crow flies down and sits on my wrist. Crows don't do that in sheep country *listen, what about THIS cat, I really wanted to know in a darkness so great I couldn't even see the walls, hell it seems ridiculous here at the breakfast table, but I was obsessed* — and suppose I ask a few people to join us because this woman is really special *wanting to know if we can IMAGINE what it's like to live in a world where every creature is a killer but if some people can be kind and the cat can't imagine that, somehow we might have the jump on him but if I'm wrong and every living thing's a killer there's no comfort in that*

— There's no comfort in that, Geoffrey.

— But it's only six people and you'll be over all that stuff by then. God, it was only a dream!

— No, I don't mean that. Dinner on Thursday's okay. Perhaps by that time I'll at least be

— You'll be fine. Jeez, that was a good breakfast! Now I'm off to the workshop to fix the engine. Sorry for the rush. See you this evening.

*

Alone in Geoffrey's cold kitchen I think of Lord Byron out there in the barn, ten thousand miles away. Our thoughts cross once again as I follow him in his shadow-patrol around the broken horse-stalls. He hears a coon-pup breathing way up in the hayloft. I follow him very closely even though, more than thirty years ago, in the paddock behind the barn, I burned his bones, burned them down to nothing.

BECAUSE MY FATHER TOLD ME, *No*
I pitched my will against the blow
of his flint mind and angry heart.
Almost four, I began the art
of silence and of cussedness.

When I was seven, with a curse
and a kindling-stick he whacked my bum
till my pants flushed with a wet flame.
The sun chilled, leaves hung dumb.
I called out. No one came.

Because my mother told me *Yes*
before I read them in a book
I guessed her reasons by her look,
and soon I learned that there were rules
older than rocks, not taught in schools.

The jacaranda bloomed: a blue shout,
louder each year, till I got out
and took to wandering, wanting to fill
my days with words, and work of hands.
Now, as I sense my slide downhill,

half-finished projects clutter my desk:
a bricolage of clips and bands.
Fall gives off a peculiar musk;
leaf-rot mixed with the stink of coons
and turkeys: mildewed afternoons.

The days get stranger: two friends die,
one in his garden, one in bed.
Smelling of pee, our fathers lie
staring at nothing, or coil up
in a tight ball over a coffee-cup.

All things have their tides and reasons:
people and trees, and these queer seasons
between two countries where I'm home
nowhere and everywhere. As I turn
gripping my hammer in my palm,

to patch the familiar roof and walls
of my house, of my self, what's gone
seems chaff in the wind. I'm on my own:
one with the coons and, I suppose,
with turkeys, and the browning rose.

Be that as it may, night spreads.
It spreads fast. I hurry outdoors
and shift my ladder along the wall.
Testing each rung, I begin my climb
through deep doorways between the stars.

David & Margaret harrison. 2021

GEOFFREY CLOSES THE DOOR of his car.

— I was in Adelaide yesterday and guess what happened.

— Tell me.

— I met someone who knew you in Melbourne years ago.

— Who?

— Fellow named Richard. Richard Hornung. He's head of the
  Flinders Street School of Music. I told him you were staying
  here at Pirra and he said: 'What? I'm driving over to see
  him,' and began packing his car. He'll be here tomorrow
  morning.

I do a quick calculation.

— My god! It must be forty years since I saw him.

— That's what he said.

Richard Hornung, ca. 2004

WHEN RICHARD STEPS INTO THE SUNLIGHT it takes me a while to catch up with the change in him. From a skinny, shy youth in a brown suit, he's filled out and is now very commanding, broad-shouldered and deep-voiced.

He tells me that he and his wife have brought nine children into the world and they are all musicians. After a third of a century we talk fast to catch up. We talk well into the night and I tell him about some of the experimental work I've been doing in poetry in performance in Minnesota and at the end of the evening he says:

— I want you to come to Adelaide and work with our students on poetry and music, in any way you like.
— Terrific. Can I try out some things on harmonic chanting and poetry? I need some students who understand music — and there are all kinds of things I want to try.

The answer's Yes. When I get back I'll send you some possible dates.

THE STUDENTS AT FLINDERS STREET School of Music are very talented. Richard and his colleagues have taught them well and soon they can hold a note and produce overtones which fill the whole body with warmth and a sense of being fully grounded. They are, however, not very well informed about poetry. So I introduce them to Hopkins, Webster, Kenneth Fearing, translations of Rilke, Pushkin, some experimental 'sound poets' such as Ernst Jandl, and some of my Australian contemporaries. We work hard on about ten poems for three weeks and they begin to delight in this new hybrid medium. Then we try out some of the poems with chanting and a few complex choral effects. For example, we take three Shakespeare songs that begin with the word 'When...' and read the songs serially, then ensemble, then as a triple canon. After several weeks we have enough pieces for an hour-long concert for a lunch-time performance at Scots' Church in the centre of Adelaide which is attended by about 150 people. To our great delight the audience responds very warmly to this new, and very old form of poetry in performance and I come away convinced that this may be an interesting alternative to the way poems are usually performed. My next task is to think about how an audience can be involved.

Helene Boucher (née Harrison) & daughter Jillian Foehn. 2021

ARMS AKIMBO IN PLUM-TREE SHADE, studying two of her thirteen grandchildren who are yelling fiercely in the garden, it's as if she's been waiting for this day all her life, and is satisfied. Helene is our sister and she wears her widowhood with dignity. She stands here like our grandparents, rooted and steady. She has made her peace with the movements of the river.

The kids come indoors and she points to the cakes and drinks she's prepared for them and they take them with delight. She asks about their recent days in school and one of them tells her several Chinese words she recently learned and how she found them very interesting and a bit amusing because you have to pronounce them very exactly. If you don't they can mean something very rude.

What the grandchildren learn from Helene is that it's very comforting to have someone really old who lives in this house not far away from theirs. It's a place where they're cherished and unconditionally welcomed. The other eleven youngsters, who are not here today, feel the same way around Helene. She is calm and benign, and she makes no fuss. She reminds me of her grandmother Lillian in Devonport, who, with Grandpa Chris, give such quiet stability to all our lives when we were kids. These kids, in their turn, respect Helene and they all talk together with great ease. In a world half-crazed with greed, drugs, money and mindless ambition such bonds gives us all a sense of richness and purpose which, with luck, will stay with us as long as we're around.

A SMALL WHITE-EYE, less than an inch, is trapped in the grape-crusher. The wheels go round and spit the bird out on the tray, among rags of grape-skin. He's almost drowned, but still cheeping loud enough to be heard above the thrum of the machine. We throw the switch and Trevor, very delicately, lifts him out. The bird's only a few bones and feathers, his skin pink and wet. He looks like a starved condor, shrunk a thousand times. Trevor takes him to the tap and washes the grape-mess away. He finds an old shoe-box, selects a worm from his fishing-box and cuts it into tiny pieces, the bird cheeping loudly all the time. Trevor feeds him, very carefully, with the worm-bits and grape-pulp. Hot with life, he gulps them down, and cheeps, and opens his beak for more.

I'm back in this orchard, which I also imagined, because I needed to. I made it up ten thousand miles away, constructed it slowly, with its rows of fruit-trees, and this river, brown and old, winding toward the coast.

*

The dream of being sucked out of a plane at 30,000 feet, and growing more conscious as you fall, comes close to the greatest horror. Even worse: the dream on the ocean floor inside a broken submarine 100 fathoms down, knowing that the last grappling-hook has snapped and you're facing your final seconds. All the oxygen's gone and neither God nor poetry can help you. Death comes at you fast like a huge wall of blackness.

You have that dream again and you wake shouting, hungering for air.

The terror is so overwhelming that it must be exorcised. As soon as I can I take my notebook and set down the lines that had been burning in my mind for months. The beginning comes easily:

Susan and Billy and Helen and me
went climbing, we got apples.
We got a bucket of sloppy lemons…

I can see the orchard and hear the kids' voices as I write, and the poem tumbles out of me in a single rush. I carry the poem across the Pacific. Today, beside the river which is swollen after rain and dark brown, I've made the last revisions and I want to tell my cousin Alison the whole story about my imagined orchard, which is also this one, where she and her family have lived so many years.

She says that would be fine, she'd like to hear it, so I say it for her:

Susan and Billie and Helen and me
went climbing, we got apples.
We got a bucket of sloppy lemons
and whammed them against the chicken-shed.
With every whump
the chickens went crazy.
Billy got sick and we showed him how
by poking your fingers down.

Helen ran home and stole some cakes
from a secret jar in her mother's place.
We went to the river and cut the rope
that tied my uncle's rowing boat
and shoved it out with a branch.
The current pulled us down a mile
before we got back to the bank.
Billy was white.

We left the boat in the mouth of a creek
and hurried home, and once I yelled:
Shut up, Susan, it was all our faults.

Behind the shed in the raspberry canes
we got undressed and looked at ourselves.
Helen's tits were bigger than Susan's.
I got all stiff and Billy tried too,
then Helen and I ran off.
I kissed her a lot in the dust and grass
and knocked her glasses off. Her little
Red thing looked like a wound and
she closed her eyes. My hand
smelt salty all afternoon.

Billy and Susan found us there,
Their eyes went down:
What were you doing, we looked for you?
'We came down here to talk for a while.
Wanna go swimming ?
Yeah, let's go !'

Susan and Billy and Helen and me
went swimming. We had the sand to ourselves.
We dived and ducked all afternoon,
we dived and ducked till the water
went like a mirror, then went black,
and we were cold — cold as a bullfrog
Billy said.

We all climbed into our pants and shirts
and raced to the shed to get our shanghais.
I heard my uncle's car in the drive
and Billy whispered, let's hide from him.

We climbed in the shed among the rafters
old tractor-bits and milk-machines
where the spiders grow. We found
a basket of mouldy eggs and a giant
freezer, and climbed in there
to hide from him.

Helen smelled salty and Susan shivered
so I held us all and kicked at the door,
and nothing moved, and I said
nothing in the dark.

Susan and Billy and Helen and me
went climbing. The apples
Shone in our hands, the lemons
bammed on the chicken-shed. And once
I swam to the top of the tree
and saw the river winding out to the sky.
Then Billy dragged me down.

                                        We slid

like fish in the yellow water and then
my uncle came and I said We
stole your apples and he looked strange
as he picked me up, his mouth was
swimming but I couldn't hear him Oh

Susan and Billy and Helen and me
went climbing the water ran fast
through the yellow apples and Susan
grabbed me and Billy screamed
we'll never — and then his breathing
stopped and the black thing came.

And then you opened the door
on Susan and Billy and Helen and me,
and then you opened the door
and Susan and Billy and Helen and me
were high in the apple-tree, and we
were dreaming.

Alison is silent after I tell her my orchard story. She drops her head but I don't know what she's thinking. She's about to say something when Trevor, grinning widely, comes to the kitchen door with the shoe-box in which the white-eye chick's bouncing about, flapping his tiny wings, insisting he will be fed, he will be heard.

LAST NIGHT, UNPACKING IN THE DARK, I left my note-book on the roof of my van. I'd driven from Alison's orchard to Noar-lunga on the coast, and the road still rocking and bumping in my body, and hungering for bed, I forgot about it. Seeing it still there on the car-roof early this morning reminded me again of the luck that's followed me all my life.

Consider what might have happened if some jogger passing by, attracted by the flashlight on top of the notebook, had taken both for his own.

All that I've said so far would have disappeared, and I'd have to re-construct it, perhaps in such a different mode the meanings would have shifted radically. That prompts me to ask a trou-bling question: Which of our verbal selves, which of my note-books—the lost one which I would have had to re-write, or this one which you're reading—should anyone believe?

The thought comes that our lives, in words, where we often spend so much of our time, are provisional. We skate on a thin ice of vowels and syllables hoping that the skin won't crack and plunge us down in the black depths, from where we might never emerge.

By what right, then, do I detain you? After all, you had no say in the transaction. It's as if, for a moment that may last an hour or more, I'm holding you by the lapel. The spaces between the words half-implore, half-command: *You are my reader. Keep reading.*

It's the same in Bristol, Jakarta—anywhere. You go into a bookshop and there we are, ranged on shelves: the writers. We offer you everything from Tibetan cooking to the history of the snow-shoe, thousands of novels, a treatise on every plant. A multitude of writers, reaching out earnestly with their versions of the world. As soon as you open any of our covers you hear the voice: *You are my reader. Read.*

Suppose you could reduce us all down to some final essence. How many of us would add a grain of wisdom to your world? You know the answer to that, and still you go on reading. Listen, the novelists say, I have a story that will take you to another place. They do not ask permission.

They take us there.

You've come home in a packed city train. You're tired. Your daughter, ill with a strange fever, is at last sleeping lightly. You pick up the new novel, a Christmas gift, lavishly reviewed, that's teased your curiosity for months. You open it. In a few seconds you're hearing voices on a large estate outside Colchester, or standing over a grave in Sian imagining the colour of ancient bones.

Why do you let yourself ride on this dragon's breath of my imagination? You're aware, most of the time, of the 'lie of literature.' All the books in this section are labelled quite plainly, if invisibly, *This is Fiction.* Yet I'm making excessive demands on your freedom. My story has an enchainment, an *engrenage* in which I shall try to enmesh you. And you enter on this contract quite willingly.

Ideally—and with false naivety—I would like you to walk out of my story as freely as you walked in, but I can't let you do that for reasons which you know as well as I.

Instead, let me pose a question.

How is it that if I write an impeccably-crafted book without much hot life—without what you might call 'a decent story' — you will smack the covers closed and destroy me? You may even bury me, fluttering, in the deep air outside your tenth-story window. If the book is merely what happened to me last Thursday or to someone else I conjured up, all our button-holing is worse than vanity. There needs to be something there beyond the lean pickings of last Thursday afternoon. It's that thing, even in the most obvious of fictions, that holds us. What is it?

In any case, why should I put off my life, neglect, for example, my daughter's fever, in order to read a hundred pages of your novel about an old man in a wheelchair mired in the gloom of himself — a gloom that came upon him even before his interminable illness? You have a confounded arrogance to presume upon my attention unless your words invoke figures and possibilities which prompt me to think more keenly about living where I am, which happens to be, right now, reading a book in this room.

Writing, we walk a Brig o' Dread: on one side Utamuro's lacquered ladies in their groomed and still perfection; on the other, incidents and emotions happening everywhere, like rain.

ON THE DINING-ROOM WALL of my old farmhouse hangs the large print of a black-and-white photo. It shows an extraordinary leap by a footballer and I have it there for several reasons, some of which I don't fully understand. The most obvious reason is pure envy. By my own calculation, in that picture, which shows a man leaping high over his opponent, his hands as they mark the football are at a great distance from the ground. It's not uncommon to see a professional basket-baller dunk the ball. To do that his hands have to reach up more than ten feet. In my print this man is at least four feet above that. The photo captures not only his athleticism but, what's more important, the sense that, *for a tiny moment, he's flying.*

The over-riding presence in the whole photo is one of elation. As in many of Matisse's dancing figures of his last great phase, the feeling it evokes is almost religious. Matisse was once asked if he believed in God and his reply was 'Only when I'm working.' My footballer, who, one imagines, was not a religious person, might have given a similar reply: 'Only when I'm doing this—when I'm flying.'

As a number of scientists with their relentless logic remind us time and again, the rate of entropy in our galaxy is increasing very fast, and not only the billions of years that it took to fashion our planet but all the work of our hands and minds will finally come to star-dust. That seems very likely.

Meanwhile, we have the span of these late days we're living in and we can, with luck, fashion something that lasts, and cannot last, and we can experience the sense of joy gifted to us by an old, disabled painter, and a young footballer, forgetting for a brief moment all the gravitas that everywhere tries to bring us down, and hold us down.

I'll keep the photo where it is.

THIS IS THE SMALLEST HOME I've ever occupied. Less than 20' long and 6' wide, stocked with all I need to sustain me. Oh, yes, Raman, I have the rice-bowl. I've also kept my Homer, two dictionaries, and several more old friends who've escaped their cardboard tombs.

I can drive my home out the gate right now. I can head off in any direction. But don't.

Instead I've parked my home under the hackberry tree. I stare at my house whose weatherboard walls seem to be vibrating under the moon. How many years have I tried to shape this house? Too many. Or was the time I've spent here exactly right?

Before turning in I jot down some ideas in the notebook I almost lost from the roof of my car in another hemisphere. Nothing useful comes. I'm looking for a rhythm, a figure I can build from.

The black dog, my old familiar, has slunk in, but this time in a comfortable shade of grey, muzzling against me. I'm almost content to have him around. My house rocks as I move along the tight corridor looking for my tooth-brush.

The moon sifts through the hackberry leaves. Mildred Overstrud planted this tree almost a hundred years ago when she was a kid, and the tree only as tall as her. She told me about it thirty years ago. Now it over-arches the house, shielding us from the sun in the summer, breaking the snow-waves in the deep of winter.

I lie down, and listen. No sound from the screech-owl. Only the faintly luminous dark in which he hunts, and hides. In the almost quiet I can hear the muffled thrum of the highway at the edge of town.

How many hours have I spent like this, lying in bed, hungering for home?

6
The Queerest Place

WHAT POURS UP FROM THE LETTER when I slit the envelope open is a flood. How could she find me here in these windy wastes when I've been so many decades away, and no words at all between us in that time?

In the next few months we make up for that silence. We write, and write and make a new beginning, but it's only a beginning.

And now the plane carrying me across the ocean is forming a bridge across the years to meet an intimate stranger.

In the seethe of the crowd in the lounge I cannot find her. Then do; the angle of her head and her firm back tell me all. She's wearing the same scarf from forty years ago on that day of wind near the Old Arts Building. The same scarf?

It cannot be.

A flurry of broken sentences and the bridge has spanned the wide water, and holds, and we're driving together through an old world of rocks and gullies and over a rough-water stream. Through an old world that I know very well and have never seen before.

DIM HYALINE PULSE OF TIDE-WATER at the mouth of the Hacking over goldgloom of sandbars then the chrysophrase depths flowing between us and under us and a fish flare cruising by, hanging there in the remembering running of how many years uncountable though the body recalls them as we roll and dive between water and air and the years stretch out between us on the sand and they say nothing then a little then more over more over more in the lifting blaze of late summer.

'These are angophora' she says one morning which I've never seen, and here, in the frame, smiling, my sons who are now far away, my sustenance specially in the time of sorrow. Polished wood-panels on the walls warmed all day by the marine sunlight and, down there, sharp white sails against the cliffs and the tide-flow that leads to the wide sea and we are somewhere near.

We are somewhere near coming home.

Jenny Gibson at her
Belconnen (Canberra) Exhibition, 2015

As Joel swings the snow-plough hard into the snow-bank then swings it away and dumps the snow on the other side of the driveway it seems as if he's been doing this for most of his life. The movements are smooth, efficient, accurate. It's the same when he trowels fresh plaster, lets it dry, then paints it, and when the thin shavings from his plane curl up and float toward the floor: the movements all have purpose.

Today we're trying to repair the cracked and sagging plaster walls in the bathroom of my old farm-house. Short of taking all the walls down and replacing the studs, floor-boards and floor, the job can't be done. We both say it almost at the same time:
— It can't be done.

The whole room's twisted by more than a hundred years of water and steam, and the piecemeal bricolage of the large original farm family which settled here over a hundred years ago, then a dozen families after that.

We stand there, staring at the cracked plaster, laughing a little.

Impossible.

'Impossible', Joel says.

He picks up a chisel.
— Let's do it.

He bangs and chisels. Bits of the wall crack off and cover the floor. He begins to laugh very loudly.

— I had an uncle in Wisconsin who always told me: *Do it right,* Joel.

More plaster breaking from the wall in even larger chunks.

Soon there are only bare studs, some of them badly twisted and behind them a few hairpins, a snapped comb and a page from a newspaper dated 1928.

Joel's still laughing and shaking his head. 'Doesn't really matter where we start. Let's do it.'

He makes tapered lathes to get the angles a little squarer, he pulls out rusted 100-year nails. It's astonishing how expertly he works.

Back at his house three miles away Joel's wife, Ritva, is preparing a meal for us which, by this time in the very late afternoon we're both beginning to taste. He says it will be some kind of Finnish dish which Ritva's mother used to cook. Joel's been lucky in marriage. His wife is graceful and intelligent, and she can really cook.

— Let's do this impossible wall, and stop for today.

We work concentratedly and fit the new plaster sheets, check the angles, nail and tape. Quicker than expected, we have the whole thing done.

—There's not one correct angle in the whole damn wall, but hell, we did it right.

He laughs outrageously.

What a delight to take these little holidays from words and lecture-rooms, where everything's complex and ambiguous. What a delight to busy one's hands, again, with the touch of *things*.

In Joel's world there are always tasks to be done immediately, and he does them, with ebullience and good humour. He has no patience for speculation. I once showed him the sketch for a sculpture I was planning. It was an almost invisible horse made of wire, leaning over a drinking trough I'd made for Katrina's pony out of an old bath-tub. I was very pleased with the whole idea and I showed Joel my sketches.

'Some people have too much time on their hands', he said.

As we get into the car we both look back. Joel's glance swivels up to the bathroom.

— Yeah, we did it right. But I still think we ought to pull your whole house down, and start again.

He's still chuckling as we take the long drive up to his house which, last year, he and Ritva designed and built with their own hands.

Brian Austen on his farm at Gisborne (Vic.) ca 2006

JUDY HAS TWO CRAFTS with a single discipline: a listening. She brings that skill, learned over many years, to everything she does. When the NAFTA agreement is first drawn up it's published in a large official book, which few read, and even fewer comprehend. At first she decides she should get a copy and study it closely. Then she has a better idea: she'll collaborate with her students and they will *all* study it for a term, compare their written notes at the end and come to a conclusion concerning the full implications of NAFTA.

She and her students set to work, and the work is difficult. After many weeks their studies show them that NAFTA is an unwieldy political legerdemain, and she and her students, very specifically, explain why.

Such work is essential in our schools, and very rare.

Her basic idea is that you teach your students by learning *with* them, an idea which is revolutionary. She adapts her strategy to suit a wide variety of purposes. It pays off every time. The students become thoroughly involved in what they're examining, they sense their responsibility, they develop as whole people. They're not, as in most schools, doing their appointed tasks only in order to write a token paper, or pass an exam.

She measures success by involvement, by genuine thinking, on her part and that of her students. They compare notes, they collaborate.

When she's not teaching she's writing poetry and prose, crafting her words with precision and purpose. She thinks with her whole body and mind. She offers many people the gift of friendship, which some of us have enjoyed for well over sixty years. She, like all of us, will die. But that thought seems very odd today as we sit on her back porch under the shade-trees enjoying a delicious Mediterranean salad which she has made with such skill, and such ease.

—AND ONE OF THEM was so fuckin good he could smell them a mile away. He'd kind of bite the air and start jumpin around and even before I stopped the pick-up he was off, and I after him fast as I could. And jeez he could run. Sometimes I'd find him way up the track and he'd have the pig by the ear, just hanging on and waitin for me, and the pig thrashin his head around bangin him against trees and rocks tryin to shake him off—but he'd hang on no matter how bad the pig bashed him. I tell you I miss that dog, he must've got me a hundred pigs, maybe more.

— What happened to him?

— Died about a month ago.

— How?

— Dunno. Just rolled over and died.

He stops, presses his lips shut and looks down at his boots.
Dead silence.

— Okay, you're there and the dog's holding onto the pig. What do you do now—shoot him?

— Nah, too dangerous. Kill your dog that way. Some shoot them. My uncle does. I go in with a knife, and stick 'em. Much better.

— Isn't *that* dangerous?

— A bit, but you get good at it. So you gut him on the spot and drag him down to the truck, and then home. Great eating, the crackling from a wild pig. I can taste it right now.

For about five years Wayne was hooked on ice—and every weekend he hunted pigs. Now he's off the ice and all he drinks is beer. But his real world is still hunting pigs.

— Wanna put some more wood on the fire? It's freezing in this pub. No heater in my room either. But I do have a fridge. Lotta good that does.

As he laughs his teeth splay out at odd angles and some are chipped and brown-edged. He sucks his beer. Gradually the fire gathers power. The big red-gum bits smoke and finally blaze up.

— You here for long?

— Maybe.

— What do you do?

— Came here to work. Trying to finish a book. I need the silence.

— Yeah this place is even quieter than Tumut. For me, the best thing about Tumut — apart from the pigs — is standin in the river and gettin a trout. The water's fast and clear, and you don't wanna fall in. Freeze your balls off. The trout are terrific. I like trout. Good little town, Tumut. I had a girlfriend there but one day she just walked out. Dunno why.

He stares at the bright logs.

After a few more minutes Wayne goes off down the long corridor to his room. He has to be up at 4.00, work in the woods until about 10.00, come back and sleep until evening. He's in charge of a machine that makes wood-chips from fallen pine-logs.

I call out good night as he goes, and poke the fire. Then I stare into it, and taste the pleasure of being alone. With Wayne's voice gone from my head the silence has become muzzy and I can't quite catch it. To find it again I go out onto the balcony. It's just after nine and the whole town's in bed. In the watery moonlight I can just make out some of the details on the hill opposite the pub. The trunks of the white sallies on the hill-flank will flare up again tomorrow, especially in the late afternoon light that pours over the roof of the pub. I gaze down the carless main street. For a moment I have the illusion that I'm the only one alive in this town.

There's not one sound in the air.

— You cold last night?

Wayne seems to have been nursing the same beer for twenty-four hours.

— No, not bad.

— Jeez, I was.

— Haven't they given you an electric blanket?

— Yeah, but I was still cold. See you got a good fire goin.

— Wanted to watch some television but there's nothing on. I tell you what, though—the other night I watched a terrific program, but I came up here a bit late and I didn't catch its name.

— What was it about?

— Bit difficult to explain, but there was this Swedish family out in the country who's heard there was a kind of huge rogue planet near the earth and everyone says it's getting closer but they can't tell for certain where it's heading. It sometimes appears in the night sky like an enormous moon, then goes away for a week or more, then comes back. The old man in the house—I think he was the father—anyway, he's terrified. He's a scientist and he seems to know more about what's happening than the others, but he still doesn't have much of a clue.

So he makes a kind of device out of a piece of cardboard, with a hole in it. You can hold it up to the planet when it swims into the night sky and if you keep it steady you can tell whether the planet's getting bigger or smaller in the hole and that tells you whether it's coming nearer, or not. One night about midnight the planet comes again and the father holds up the cardboard to it, then, without saying anything, he hands the piece of cardboard to his kids. He goes downstairs and we don't see him again. We learn later he'd run to the basement and shot himself. Anyway, when he'd gone, the three others in the family hold up the viewer

213

and the white planet's growing like mad and then, very suddenly, it reverses and floats back into the dark. They're all relieved and go to bed.

— Jeez, that sounds weird. What happened then?

— Well, the next night, the family sees this unbelievable light in the sky. They look at it through the cardboard and again it's expanding really fast. At the same time the air's getting colder and leaves and branches are flying about and none of the family knows what to do, so they all go out onto the lawn. Maybe it seemed safer out there. I don't know. Anyway, it wasn't safer. All we see is this big white planet coming down right on the house — and at the same time the whole world's getting colder and colder and by this time I can hardly watch the screen and I'm on my feet looking at their terrified faces and the blazing white of the landscape and the trees thrashing about — bits of tree, flying everywhere. And then the whole film finishes in a kind of chaos of sounds I'd never heard before, and this is the really strange thing — in the last moment there's a huge flash and a complete white-out and I'm left staring at a white television screen. Everything's blank white.

— What are you telling me all this for? It sounds really mad and I'm fuckin glad I didn't see it.

— I know. Since I saw it I can't get it out of my mind. The other night when it was full moon it seemed like the landscape here was just like the one in the film and it got me thinking.

— Jeez, it would make me want to stop thinking and grab a beer. In fact I'm gonna do that right now. Want one?

— No thanks. I'm off it for the moment.

Wayne goes to his room and fetches a beer.

In his absence I'm beginning to think I should shut up now. I manoeuvre another log into the fire. Wayne comes back and sits with his head bent toward the flames.

At last he breaks the silence.

— Well, what did you think about after that crazy film?

— Lots of things. For starters I thought about how long we humans have been on this planet?

— What's that got to do with anything?

— Well, most scientists think it's about 200,000 years but that's nothing compared to the age of the planet—which is supposed to be over 4 billion years—and the first inhabitants of this country, who we've been trying to wipe out since we came, have been here possibly 60,000 and even that's almost nothing in the whole span of time since the beginning. Human life, in time, is *very* close to nothing.

— So?

— Well, the film made me feel how incredibly unimportant we are. Here, at Captain's Flat I began to see that clearly for the first time. It has something to do with what I've been reading too. Imagine just after the Big Bang—there must have been stretches of time when it was like tonight for billions of years. I can't get my head around that.

— Me neither.

— And it wasn't until I came here to this pub in Captain's Flat that I began to understand anything about what we're doing in the little bit of time we have left. There's something peculiar about this town. You're cutting logs and shooting pigs and I'm trying to write a book and we're both surrounded by this silence which I've never really heard before, and it sometimes scares the daylights out of me.

Wayne looks at me rather oddly. I can sense that, though his body's quite still, he's edging away from me inside and he really wants to be somewhere else.

— You're not a nancy boy are you?

— I don't think so. I'm just trying to get used to the Australian countryside, which I thought I knew. This is a helluva place to do it. And what I'm learning is that I know almost nothing, and it doesn't really matter what I do but I have to do it all the same. It's giving me a lot to think about—this place and that film. A lot.

Once again, we fall into a long silence.

— Has anyone ever told you that you're a bit nuts?
— Quite often. My family used to look at me and call me a 'rum fellow!' That's one of the reasons I left Australia. Apparently there were so many weird people where I was going that no one would notice me. Maybe that's why I had a great time overseas. Now I'm back and I don't really know where I am—but I like the uncertainty.
— Yeah, I felt like that in Sydney last year. I thought I'd lost it. Couldn't even remember my name—maybe I'd been using too much ice—anyway I found myself peeing out of a hotel window onto a taxi. Maybe you better get off whatever it is you're into.
— Perhaps. But I don't know what I'm into.
— All this stuff about planets and mad films—is that what you're writing about?
— Not really, I'm writing about some of the things and people I've met, and lately about this town. I want to write a book anyone can read. I don't write difficult stuff, and I don't think I'm mad, but I sure as hell can't be too certain about it.

Again, a long silence during which whatever planet out there is waiting to wipe us all out doesn't arrive. It seems the world isn't ending yet. Or, if it is, no one's taking any notice.

WHEN I WAKE IN THE DARK and shuffle, half-asleep, along the pub corridor toward the bathroom, the silence which seems to belong to Captain's Flat has thickened. Wayne's light is on and his door flung wide. He's almost dressed and ready for work on his wood-chip machine up in the hills. As I pass his room he calls out:

— Hey, that story you told me last night gave me nightmares — I couldn't fuckin sleep.

'Sorry about that Wayne', I mutter. 'I thought that…'

— And I got to wondering why in hell you have to think and talk about all that stuff.

He approaches me, eyes glaring.

— Maybe you'd better take a long holiday or something. You told me your family used to think you were a bit nuts, and maybe they were right. You might need some help.

He turns away, then twists around

— I'm going crackers too. Don't tell me any more about that stuff. I can't stop thinking about it.

He drops down the stairwell and lunges out into the dark: 'You need to go for a long drive, or do some fishin, or something.'

Could be, I mutter into the dark stairwell. *Could be.*

BRIAN FALLS OVER BACKWARD in an English hospital and the rupture in his neck-bone releases a flood of staphlococci that partly paralyses him. He cannot lift his arms very well and now they've removed eight seats from the plane that carries him out of England and is bringing him home.

Back here in Melbourne he's slumped over awkwardly in a special chair. He's still unable to raise his arms, one of which is covered in plaster, and he's in pain. Nonetheless he greets me with warmth and enthusiasm before he tells me his story. In spite of everything it's a joyful meeting, and we talk on for some time.

At last I ask him: 'Well, Brian, what's the plan from here?'

He hesitates, then he looks me in the eye. The old blue steel's still flashing there:
— Mate, I'm gonna walk out of here.
— Good on you.

We talk on for quite a while, our thoughts crossing and re-crossing, and our words jumbling, cohering, again jumbling. Then, as I'm leaving I call back while he gives an awkward nod: 'See you in a few days!'

As I make my way to the car I'm racked with contending feelings. *I don't think he'll be walking out of that place soon. Maybe not ever,* I say to the air. At the same time I'm once again astonished at the guts that Brian's showing, as he has so many times before. He's almost a cripple but his will's indomitable and I find myself crying in gratitude for this long friendship. I even experience a fugitive flash of envy.

Brian's determined to do something about his condition.

It will take us both some time to find out exactly what it will be.

R 20

Christina at 80

6.30 A.M. HEAVY THUMPS ON THE VAN. *'Five minutes to get out. Five minutes! We've got to go! Now!'*

A huge sea-wind's crashing into the trees all around us.

I thrash the sheet away from my body and hurl myself into the driver's seat, loosen the hand-brake and let the van roll back down the makeshift ramp we made last night. Then I turn the wheel hard uphill. Jenny sprints into the house and gathers some clothes, and a book. There's already a horrible yellow and blood-red glow spreading in the trees at the top of the rise. That's exactly where we're heading. I start the engine but none of the low gears will engage, so I try third, and manage to ram it in, then drive five yards up the slope, slowly, slipping the clutch for a full minute, willing the clutch-plate not to burn out. The van judders to a stop.

'Three to go', yells Mark, *'It's coming right at us.'*

I shove my foot down hard on the clutch and this time engage second gear and coax the van as fast as I dare up the muddy track. The flare in the trees now covers the horizon and we can feel waves of heat belting us and we haven't yet reached the boundary road that will take us out, beyond the trees. When we do, just in time, we meet Jenny's two sons, Mark and Tom who, along with their children and Aurelia, Tom's partner, have been waiting very anxiously for us to join them, and they all jump into their cars, and head, with us close behind them, down to the beach, very fast. It only takes a few seconds for the fire to leap the road behind us and set the gorse and spotted gums on the family property ablaze.

*

An enormous woman with two cats in two cages, yowling in the smoke haze; she's unable to make much progress across the sand. We help her shuffle herself and her cats toward the shoreline. The terrified cats try to claw their way out. Five yards away there's another woman trying to control her horse, which turns in crazed circles as the crowd on the beach thickens and the horse, terrified, keeps jerking its head up, trying to shake off its halter.

*

When I gaze into the blackening air I make out a headland which turns, immediately, into smoke. If we're forced off the beach there's no escape but the open ocean. The two headlands enclosing the beach are like the legs of a giant crab already flickering with yellow shoots and explosions, and the air's gone dark with a wide glow of crimson along the horizon.

We fashion makeshift smoke-masks and some people are coughing, hard, and shoving their heads into sweaters and blankets.

No one has seen this film before but we've all seen the trailers. But this time we are the film and all our actions are unscripted and they all feel wrong. We hardly speak to each other and there are now hundreds of us on the beach all witnessing whatever it is we've been cast for. It's amazing how stunned, and how half-automatic our actions are. By late afternoon we're marooned on a beach in this little bay, the coast road blocked both ways. How many days of food in the country store?

We study our flimsy possessions. Enough clothes to keep the evening cold away but tonight there'll be no evening cold. We sit there watching mothers, trying to hide their terror, digging about in bags and boxes for something to feed their children.

*

Rebecca harrison. 2020

DAVID SQUINTS DOWN THE PIECE OF WOOD he's just sawn and sanded in his vise and his expression and movements bring back the way our father went about his tasks in the workshop. He takes his time. He wants to get it right. As he hands me the piece he's devised for my van so many memories spring up it's difficult to sort them out. He's in his nineties now and I'm trying to make the images coalesce. Was this the brother I tried to drown in the Hawkesbury so many years ago, and who's been on my conscience ever since? It can't be, and it is. I've tried to write about it in an attempt to purge the memory. I've talked to friends and counsellors trying to understand, and nothing has made much difference.

Since that time in the river, much of which I've spent in other countries, David's fathered five children and now he has a whole brood of grandkids. We've both suffered the death of a daughter; we've worked long years at the demanding craft of teaching, tried to play golf, and lived our lives as richly and as well as we can. It's impossible to say how successful we've been. That's for someone else, or no one, to determine. For my own part, I can say that, were I a Christian man, I wouldn't be over-eager to face a reckoning with my Maker right now.

What I can say about David, and his wife Margaret is that they have kept their sanity and their sense of quiet purpose and their strong bonds with their large and still-burgeoning family. They have endured and they are enduring.

David hands me the piece of wood he's shaped for me. 'There, that should do the job', he says. He picks up his drill and some torx screws and we both go outside, find the spot in the van where the wood-bracket goes. We measure carefully, then drill holes and fix it exactly in its proper place.

HE'S UP EARLY. The second volume of his memoir will be launched later today, and he's preparing savoury dips for the guests. After ten minutes on the phone he's told me what he's been up to for the last week or so, and I'm dizzy with the sheer volume of the stuff he accomplishes. A few months ago he turned 91. This year, he's also gathered, in three volumes, the scores of all the works he wrote for the students who came to his music-schools at Pirra Arts Centre back in the eighties and nineties. Today, at his launching he'll play a flute improvisation. It's dancing in his mind as he cooks, but he doesn't want to fix the run of it too exactly as that would spoil the whole idea of inventing the music as he performs it. That's the fun of it.

These days, when he can't sail, he's reading *all* of Jane Austen. He's done the same with Sir Walter Scott. Geoffrey reads his chosen authors *in toto*, even James Joyce—including the (to me) incomprehensible *Finnegan's Wake*—which no one else I know, except Anthony Burgess, has ever finished. 'It's verbal music' he says. 'I don't worry about it. I let it flow.'

Even his much younger friends can't keep pace with Geoffrey. He's the same dynamo I met in high-school 75 years ago and have held as a solid friend ever since. Although he doesn't leap the high hurdles any more, the energy of his imagination is undiminished. He has scores of friends in Australia and Ireland and he's made a wide-ranging contribution to musical life in both countries—as a composer, a performer and a superlative teacher. In his tenth decade, like Walt Whitman, he's still open to all that life offers. A few weeks ago he began writing his first novel and he still relishes playing flutes from many countries, as well as sackbutts, krumhorns and marimbas. He builds boats, cooks the best *moules marinières* I've ever tasted; he plays 'boules', brews stout and cider, and on and on.

He tells me the new novel is well down the skids. That will be his sixth book for the year. After all, it's only June.

WE DON'T KNOW WHEN CHRISTINA will die but it will be soon. In the quietest way she has made her peace and, as usual, she is resolved. After the years of digging in the river-flats and plains of Minnesota and countless hours hunched over the screen, writing technical reports on her findings, Christina's bones are fast crumbling.

We take shifts to be with her. Today I'm alone with her and she's trying to say something which I can't make out. I lean closer and, as I do, her faint voice becomes a little stronger:

We never   talked

The words are clear but soft. I lean closer.

I wanted   explain

Maybe... maybe... it's best for you to keep your strength, Christina

No, no   Please no   words

Please   listen

She falls back deeper into her pillow and I wait for many minutes and wonder if she's sunk, again, into the coma that's held her several days

quite suddenly she turns toward me

I didn't leave   because

long pause   her breathing coming hard

It wasn't
            I had to try

my own

Christina, can I say…

no, not   I have   there's   more

She's breathing very evenly. Her eyes are closed and this time the pause seems interminable

I take her hand and the silence gathers round us for minute on minute

She falls into a deeper silence and I'm not sure she can hear me as I say very slowly

so many things, Christina
                              I'm sorry…
and, while I'm trying to speak, very slowly, and very firmly, her fingers tighten round my hand.

Just once.

Then she lets go.

THE DREAM-WORDS STILL ENTIRELY CLEAR in the starlit dawn, '*Sovegna vos*', and I'm startled, as I sit on the bed's edge, to find myself beginning to cry, then more words come back from the dream, just as clearly, *Lasciate ogni speranza…* and upright now, lost in bewilderment and the tears barely holding back because our daughter, Rebecca, has been ill these many years and is very ill today and far down in a terrible darkness and cannot tell what's true and what a chimera, and her little dog also ill from a mysterious concussion. Did someone hurl her tiny, helpless companion against a wall, and where do the words 'brain-damaged' belong here in this welter of images which come flooding across the Pacific pulling my whole being down into an anxious nausea which never goes away? Is everyone brain-damaged, here in this vast empire of money and noise, and now the words come back again, *Sovegna vos*, from Arnaut Daniel in his long fall into hell: *Sovegna*, with a drenching sadness, as grey sunlight filters through the parkland trees and now we're walking about the rooms in our heads looking for something which also has no name as we try to send each other gifts over the huge dividing ocean, two words, with a space before and after, *Sovegna vos*, and not knowing why we send them except they must be spoken at this time,

Sovegna vos a temps de ma dolor,

again and again, into the troubled air of this long pre-morning and pre-mourning.

DEAR KATRINA: This is a helluva time to write you a birthday letter. It seems our worlds are in permanent lockdown and neither of us may be allowed to move from where we are for months, maybe even more. From where I am now everything tells me that the American Empire, or whatever we like to call it, is fast crumbling. Rampant Capitalism has almost destroyed itself and, in the larger world, so many leaders are pursuing dictatorial policies that one comes away from reading about present events feeling sick and dizzy with despair. So many of us are displaced, starving, homeless and desperately ill, that there's little excuse for those of us who are more fortunate for any rejoicing.

In spite of that here is what I want say to you: for many years, you have been the lynch-pin of this family and none of us have given you anything like the honour you deserve. While your mother was going through her last two painful years you were always there, paying attention to her every need. When she was in her own house next door you were constantly there, tending to her very difficult and demanding cats, feeding her, attending to all her finances and performing all the other chores that in her illness and disorientation, she was beginning to neglect. At the same time you were trying to support your own family. Not once did you complain under that extremely demanding bur-den. I helped where I could, and it wasn't much.

Added to all that, for years before your mother's illness you had been looking after your sister in her very stubborn and long addiction. She mostly gave you hell, but you understood the nature of her illness and you forgave her. That went on for years and when your mother was losing her grip on life you kept steady and cared for both of them in so many ways that, as I look back, it fills me with amazement.

It has been difficult for me, until today, to write anything about Rebecca and even now I am so desolated by what happened to the fine young woman who had all the opportunities to lead a healthy and worthwhile life. The waste was a devastation for everyone who knew her. Our love for her was simply not enough. There was probably something at the root of her self-destruction which I will never understand and I will keep on wondering about it, and intermittently blaming myself for her fate and conjecturing what more I could have done, until the end of my own time. I know you share some of my puzzlement and horror and sadness, so part of what I want to say on your birthday is to re-assure you: you did everything in your very considerable power to put yourself between Rebecca and her destruction and in the end, whatever it was that was afflicting her, it was just too strong for all of us. So many people tried to help her, and you were chief among them. But she had made up her mind that it was all just too difficult for her. As you said a number of times, it was her choice, and one has to respect it.

I think in adopting a positive strategy for dealing with our loss we have found a way, in these last dark months, to cope. Rebecca, at her best, was a thoughtful and politically aware person, and though I'm temperamentally not attuned to political activism, and have much else to do, as a tribute to her, I'm putting my shoulder to a few minor political wheels, while I have time and energy to do so. Another way I'm trying to be useful is engaging with as many people as I can in solid political discussions. She liked that, and she brought to it an admirable wit and compassion.

There is much more to say on all this and we'll get a chance to do that in the fullness of time.

Meanwhile, I want to tell you how delighted I am that, after all these months and months of separation, the disease that still threatens all of us has abated perhaps enough to let you come, at last, for a visit across the wide water. That would be a wonderful birthday present for me as I round the corner of my tenth decade and (perhaps too early) I'm counting the days. But I haven't finished. For your birthday, I wanted to let you know that this time of bereavement has been so difficult for me that, without your constant care and compassion I doubt that I would have made it. There have been some days when I was close to being crazed with sorrow, but you were always there holding steady and steering us all, and yourself, through an intolerable season. So let's rejoice in your birthday however we can, in spite of all the darkness which threatens to surround us for some time yet. You have been and are the finest daughter any man could wish for and there is no way I can fully express my gratitude for all you've done for me, and for all of us.

Dad

Home by myself in my draughty house,
November snow splatting down:
We stuff that slides off the apple-boughs.
Two nights ago I stopped a fat raccoon
in the headlights as
he toppled a trash-can: black
ears of a fox, and jewel eyes
white-circled like a clown's.
Then he melted back
into the sleeve of darkness. Today I look
for a hairy smudge on the white
page of the paddock.
Nothing — only the snow-plain
spreading all around. This quiet —
save for the squeak of my wet finger
against the window-pane —
is ten miles thick.

And so I welcome myself to my house again.
I built this bed —
great yawning thing
too vast for any couple, three times too wide
for a bachelor's narrow sleep;
built it of pitch-pine and cheap
plywood, bought
at a country auction, years ago.
the bolts don't match. I've knocked it
apart too often — once in Toronto,
twice for garrets in this town.

Now it's grown
Into the conscience of the house — not
grafted, though, to any olive-root, nor
decked with damasks of Indian-tooth design.

Oddly, the sherbet-bearers who used to float
at evening through the door
to lay me down and soothe my limbs with oils
from Nineveh and Samarkand
don't come by any more.
Being too idle to unbolt the thing again
I shall maybe die in it,
but maybe not today.
                              Above it, a great
painting by Pieter de Hooch:
a woman and a snivelling kid
in a courtyard, 1658.
Deftly placed, every flag and brick
burns clear in the moist light. The broom,
obedient to the painter's fabulating eye,
leans correctly on the wall.

The courtyard door frames
a second woman. White
paper surrounds them all.
The print's buckled, it curls from the masonite.
The whole thing's wrongly
angled.
                              Beside it
the window frames the golf-hut
from where all summerlong they putt
on the opulent green. Summer's gone underground;
the workmen keep indoors today, honing
purple hands.
                              Here I am, in my
middle years, in the wastes of white
America. Something has slid away.
I wait for the voices of my daughters—who might
flounce in, snow in their hair,
any week now. Meanwhile, it's me
and the raccoon—he's out there somewhere, surely.

Home, but not quite Ithaka, where the waves
churn shingle up the yellow shore —
Not quite, not quite. But since —
pace the story of your
perpetually renewable Ulysses, who,
after the thrumming of the harp had stopped
and all the color drained from the day, propped
himself against that olive-root
and fought the queer taste
that thickened in his throat
and died unsinging, a prince
of absences — since
I have chosen
to arrange things in this way,
I am the husband of these frozen
fruit-trees, these minutes
that drip from the eaves
and it seems, quiet mister,
that it must do, it must
exactly do.

EPILOGUE

for Jenny

If water. And a red stone, red bird breathing in the branches, staring down. If water, sliding over veined rock in a pulse of sunlight, over our bodies in the water and bright beads flung skyward from our hands. If water comes like this, then surely. Bubbles across our bodies, sun-froth. Look down at the signings of the years: puckers, strength drawn away, as from horses in their uphill furrows. Darker voicings now. Further down, tread gingerly, not skip over stones in the starved creek-bed, waiting for rain. This ageing, this wearing down also a form of fire. And if it comes as a being it is always a being here, among flames in the waratah, banksia-cones, smooth sleep of angophora limbs. Rub our hands against their skins and agree, if water, then surely to love each other is merely a flowing and a letting go.

PERSONAE

Numbers indicate the page of first appearance

Lex Banning 77
Larry Adler, 13
W. H. Auden, 85
Brian Austen, 43
Diane Austen, 59
J. S. Bach, 162
George Barker, 90
Joel Barsness, 206
Ritva Barsness, 207
Norm Beckham, 30
Phyllis Beckham, 30
Martin Bell, 101
John Betjeman, 85
William Blake, 54
Bob Bonner, 150
Helene Boucher, 14
Alf Brookes, 13
Vincent Buckley, 144
Malcolm Calley, 64
Wolf Clutterbuck, 6
Geoffrey D'Ombrain, 25
Judith Daniel, 210
Arnaut Daniel, 228
Marlene Dietrich, 100
T. S. Eliot, 55
Ron Fitzgerald, 41
Dorothy ("Dottie") Gerasimo, 163
Jenny Gibson, 56
Mark Gibson, 221
Laila Haglund, 64
Britt Haglund, 97
Harvey Hall, 86
Lord Harewood, 85
Max Harris, 95
Jess Gladys Harrison, 3
David Harrison, 5
Harvey Harrison, 5
Christopher John Harrison, 36
Lillian Caroline Harrison, 36

LOCALES

Northcote, Victoria,
Windsor, N.S.W
Sydney, N.S.W: various places
Balwyn, Box Hill, Melbourne, Victoria
M.S. Skaubryn en route to Southhampton
London, various places
Edinburgh,
Iowa City, Iowa
'Hackberry Hollow', Northfield, Minnesota
Minneapolis, Minnesota
Pirra Arts Centre, Lara, Victoria
Bundeena, N.S.W.
Melbourne University, Melbourne
Mungo Park, Lake Mungo N.S.W
Adelaide, S.A.
Captain's Flat, N.S.W.
Near Willaura, Victoria
St. Paul, Minnesota
Bubbling Springs Farm, near Menomonie, Wisconsin
Malua Beach, near Bateman's Bay, N.S.W.

NOTES

1. Kookaburra Kanon, page 157. The piece is written to be performed twice, once solo, then as a canon. The second voice begins two beats after *Hey, Jack. The piece should be performed in fairly strict metronomic time with allowances for a wide range of volume, emphasis and tone to suit individual performers. In bar two of the last line it will be evident that the first voice has to delay so that the second voice can catch up. The delay can be performed effectively by the first voice saying the sound 'ka' in strict time until both voices pause for two beats and then say, ensemble and quite loudly, the last 'Hey Jack!'

2. The poem "Susan and Billie and Helen and me" on page 195 which has been published elsewhere with the title BALLAD, has a curious genesis which needs some explanation. My old friend, Michael Dennis Browne, years ago came back from a poetry reading on the east coast and told me of a poem he'd heard which was about the death of four children on a farm in, as I remember, Iowa. The poem terrified and angered me so much that over a period of months I couldn't shake it out of my mind. My mistaken sense was that Michael didn't know who wrote the poem and I had, I believed, no way of finding out. One day, at my desk, some lines jumped into my head and, animated by the same terror that Michael's original re-telling had prompted in me, I very quickly wrote down my version of the story with the sole aim of getting it out of my head, and setting myself free of it. A few days later I rang Michael and told him what I'd done. He was appalled, and informed me that the poem he'd told me about was by Roland Flint. Very surprised, I wrote almost immediately to Roland Flint explaining what I'd done. That was many years ago. I heard nothing from him in the intervening years and have looked in all the books published in his name and have never found the poem. Roland Flint has been dead these many years now so I don't have, and will possibly never have any idea, beyond Michael's re-telling, of how my version compares with his.

www.ingramcontent.com/pod-product-compliance
Lightning Source LLC
Chambersburg PA
CBHW070328090426
42733CB00012B/2406